Quarterback Play
Fundamentals and Techniques

Ron Jenkins

ISBN: 1-58518-601-5
Library of Congress Control Number: 2001098599

Book layout: Jennifer Bokelmann
Diagrams: Ron Jenkins
Cover design: Kerry Hartjen
Front cover photo: Jed Jacobsohn/Getty Images

Coaches Choice
P.O. Box 1828
Monterey, CA 93942
www.coacheschoice.com

DEDICATION

This book is dedicated to my nephew Justin Jenkins — a great kid!

ACKNOWLEDGMENTS

I would like to thank the following quarterbacks who I have worked with over the last few years as their quarterback coach. They bought into my coaching philosophy and style and trusted me with their careers. I learned a great deal from their feedback and our open exchanges over the last seven years.

Chris Kastillar – Santa Monica College (1994 – 95), San Jose State University

Marcus Grundy – Santa Monica College (1994 – 95), Howard University

Jack Hawley – Los Angeles Harbor College (1996 – 97), San Diego State University

Terrence Johnson – Los Angeles Harbor College (1997 – 98), Alabama State University

Phillip Reed – Los Angeles Harbor College (1999), West Virginia Tech

Ryan Gilbert – El Camino College (2001), Northern Illinois University

Ron Venters – El Camino College (2002)

Ugo Felizzola – El Segundo High School (2002)

Jordan Tusieseina – Redondo Union High School (2002)

CONTENTS

INTRODUCTION

The quarterback position is the cornerstone of any modern offense. Unfortunately, there are not enough naturally gifted athletes around to play the position effectively enough to win on a consistent basis. Therefore, coaching fundamentally sound mechanics to your quarterbacks is essential to the increased success of your offense. Brad Oates of ESPN writes, "The secret to (Mike) Holmgren's successful system for coaching quarterbacks is preparation. Nothing is left to chance. Mechanics such as footwork and throwing motion are heavily scrutinized on every play in practice and in games. The coaches demand precision at all times. Game preparation is exhaustive and the quarterbacks are heavily involved."

In addition (and I think this is extremely important), coaches can teach their quarterbacks to think about how they are thinking (metacognition). In other words, most quarterbacks need to be taught a strategy, or a process of thinking, that will greatly enhance their success on the football field. The most basic, yet complex, strategy a quarterback can learn is the pre-snap read, in which the quarterback will eliminate some of his passing options (due to the defender's leverage or the specific coverage) before the ball is snapped. This will help the quarterback make quick, decisive decisions with greater success.

This book will give the reader a more thorough understanding of the techniques, mechanics, and thought processes required to play the position of quarterback at the high school or college level. It was written for coaches, players, as well as for those parents who are interested in providing the athlete with the fundamental skills necessary to play quarterback to the best of their individual abilities.

This book will provide most of the information necessary to teach the athlete how to play quarterback efficiently and effectively. Every subject covered and every drill discussed is important in the development of the quarterback at every level of play. Hard work on the mechanics and techniques can measurably develop a quarterback's consistency.

It is especially important that the quarterback utilize sound technique and mechanics in the passing phase of the offense. This is because poor technique causes injuries to quarterbacks consistently. Quarterbacks often experience problems with their shoulders, elbows, arms, and forearms because they are using poor mechanics when passing the football. Just one acute flaw will force the quarterback to counterbalance the throwing motion with another flaw. For example, a quarterback cannot throw the ball using a sidearm motion without some kind of counter motion elsewhere in his mechanics.

Although teaching sound mechanics takes time and effort, it's always well worth it. When a quarterback uses good technique and mechanics, he can throw more passes and experience much less fatigue, thus greatly reducing his chance of injury. In addition, the quarterback will increase his accuracy. Accuracy in passing comes from balance; and the quarterback's feet produce balance.

This book also presents a simple and descriptive way to teach and learn the proper skills that will enable an athlete to be as effective and efficient as possible playing quarterback. Specific drills will be given that can be used to learn and refine each particular technique.

A few of the drills explained in this book are designed to "overemphasize" a certain skill in order to retrain the quarterback's muscle memory. An example might be a "shoulder-spin" drill that will have the quarterback overrotate his torso so that the back of his throwing shoulder ends up facing the target. Even though a quarterback would rarely, if ever, follow through to such an extent, this drill would illustrate to the quarterback how it feels to follow through in such a way that it would improve his mechanics from a technical standpoint, which would allow him to throw a better pass.

This book is broken down into chapters that will cover specific topics or skills. You can go through the book from start to finish to learn what is necessary in playing the position well, or use the book as a reference guide to troubleshoot areas of concern. It also discusses quarterback mechanics and techniques that are necessary from the moment he approaches the line of scrimmage to the end of the football play, going through each technique in the order it usually comes up in any specific play.

As each technique and mechanic is discussed, a drill is usually provided to teach the technique to the player. Hopefully, the written description, along with the picture and or diagram, will provide the clarity necessary to teach and learn the skill effectively.

It is my hope that this book will assist coaches and quarterbacks make their offenses more efficient and productive. The best way to teach these techniques and skills would be to utilize the four laws of learning: explanation (by the coach), demonstration (by the coach or by the use of film), imitation (by the player), and many, many repetitions by the player himself.

My suggestion is that as you learn these techniques and drills, you should start out slowly and build up the speed as you master the skills. Start off walking through the techniques, then go to half speed, and then to full speed. Once you have truly learned the techniques, you will be able to execute them full speed during a game with no problem; they will become second nature to you.

Summary of Introduction

- Only a limited number of naturally gifted quarterbacks are available for every team.

- It's extremely important to teach quarterbacks a strategy or a process of thinking that will enhance their success on the field.

- Teaching fundamentally sound mechanics to your quarterbacks will increase the success of your offense.

- Sound mechanics and technique greatly reduce injuries to the quarterback's arm.

- This book will give a more through understanding of quarterback techniques.

- This book is written for coaches, players, and parents.

- Every subject, technique, and drill in this book is important in developing quarterbacks.

- This book presents a simple and descriptive way to teach and learn the skills necessary to become a more effective quarterback.

- This book is broken down into chapters to cover specific topics or skills.

- The mechanics will be explained in the order they occur in any given play.

- While discussing the skill, a drill will usually be given to teach and learn the skill.

- When learning these skills, start off by walking through them and then build up speed as you learn the techniques.

Things to Look for in a Quarterback

- Instinct is the most important factor.
    - √ Knowing who to throw to, given the defense or match-up.
    - √ Being able to anticipate when to release the pass before the receiver makes his break.
    - √ Having the ability to sense pressure and avoid it while focusing downfield.
- Vision: the ability to see the whole field in a given play.
- The ability to make all the appropriate throws in a given offense is much more important than being able to throw the football a hundred yards.
    - √ Accuracy is more important than arm strength.
        - ◆ If the offense is comprised of short to intermediate passes, the completion percentage should be at least 60%.
        - ◆ The touchdown to interception ratio should be at least 2:1.
    - √ A quarterback never has to throw the ball more than 60 yards.
- Quick feet (which is very different from speed), agility, and the ability to avoid rushers are very important.
- An innate desire to compete.
- At some point, everyone gets down on a quarterback. So the quarterback's belief in himself must be unwavering. The more sensitive he is to criticism, the more this will compound his problems.
- Height and speed should be looked at as potential bonuses in a quarterback.

Things to Remember as a Quarterback

- Always keep your eyes on your target (not on the flight of the ball) when the ball is in the air.
  - √ This increases your accuracy dramatically over time.
- Never throw late over the middle.
  - √ The pass will likely be intercepted.
- Never take a sack in the quick passing game.
  - √ Learn how to just throw the ball away.
- Always finish a hand off.
  - √ It sets up your play-action passes.
- Never take a sack on third down when you're within field goal range.
  - √ Just throw the ball away.
- Physically learn how to throw each individual pass route.
  - √ Every individual pass route is a different type of throw. For example, throwing a 12-yard speed-out to the wide receiver is very different from throwing a delay route to the back four-yards downfield from the line of scrimmage, which in turn is very different from throwing streak route down the sideline.
- Always get to the line of scrimmage quickly with your hands under the center.
  - √ Now the defense has to show you what defense they are going to run.
  - √ If they stem, they have to do it right away.
    - ◆ You now have time to change the play without getting a delay of game penalty.
- Always vary your snap count.
  - √ This can aid in controlling the rush.
    - ◆ This can keep the blitz off you because defenders have to either show you they are blitzing right away, or they will get a late start after you have the football, because they can't anticipate the snap.
    - ◆ This can also give your linemen a jump on their blocks because the defense has to stay in their stances until the ball is moved, rather than anticipating the snap of the ball.

CHAPTER 1

The Dropback-Passing Game

Introduction

One of the most basic teaching principles in the dropback-passing game is the creation of a rhythm between the quarterback's drop and the receiver's break. The quarterback should be able to unload the football just as the receiver is breaking open. This capability will help the linemen execute their blocks and will help put the ball into the receiver's hands the instant he separates from the defender.

The ability to control his drop so that he reaches the end of it just as the receiver is about to break open is a cornerstone of efficient quarterback play. Usually, this means that the quarterback should employ a controlled drop and glide back rather than rush or hurry back in a violent manner.

When a quarterback sprints back too fast, he has to be just as violent in trying to stop himself. When this occurs, it's very hard to be balanced and have his shoulders level for the throw, or to have any rhythm with the receiver. When a quarterback glides back, he creates a rhythm in his drop and in his throw, and he's able to see things downfield more clearly and throw the ball more effectively in an efficient, smooth manner. It is imperative that the quarterback be in a position to see the entire field during his drop.

Additionally, by throwing the football precisely at the end of the drop, the offensive line is better able to control the rush of the defenders. When quarterbacks hurry their drops, they end up having trouble with their mechanics because they are usually off-balance when the try to throw the pass. Many times when they do get to the end of their drops, they have to wait for the receivers to break open. Often they will be just standing back there getting tense while the rushers have an aiming point. Once the quarterback hits the end of his drop, the rushers can really push upfield toward them.

When a quarterback glides back, hits the end of his drop, and releases the pass, the defenders eventually let up right away. In fact, later on in the game, you will notice that when this type of quarterback hits the end of his drop, the rushers usually let up, even when the quarterback is hitching up in the pocket to throw. The quarterback has trained the defense to realize that the ball is gone as soon as the he hits the last step in the drop. Creating this rhythm can really have an effect on the pass rush.

This type of drop allows the quarterback to begin reading the coverage right away as he is dropping back to pass. Some quarterbacks don't really begin to make their decisions until they are at the end of the drop. Frequently, the quarterback will run out of time because he can't take in all the information in such a short period of time. By reading the defense as he is dropping back, the quarterback can anticipate what the coverage is going to do. It's much easier when the quarterback gets a good pre-snap read based on the leverage of defenders, and then read the defense during the drop so he can anticipate when the receiver will break open. But to accomplish all of this, the quarterback must have sound mechanics from the start.

Summary of the Dropback-Passing Game

- The quarterback should be able to unload the football just as the receiver is breaking open.
- A cornerstone of efficient quarterback play is the ability to control the drop so he can time out the throw.
- Hurrying the drop will result in bad mechanics.
- The quarterback needs to be able to see the entire field during the dropback.
- Throwing the football as the quarterback hits the end of his drop helps the pass protection.
- A controlled drop allows the quarterback to read the coverage immediately and throughout the drop, which will help him anticipate what the defense is attempting to do.
- A controlled drop requires sound, efficient mechanics.

Body- and Foot-Action Terms

The following terms are normally used with respect to the body and foot action of the quarterback when he is passing the football. These terms are important in that they explain how the quarterback should position his feet and body when throwing a pass. The proper positioning of the quarterback's feet and body are extremely critical if he wants to throw an accurate pass with good rotation and the proper velocity.

Compact (as in *staying compact*): This means that the quarterback has a good bend at the knees in his drop, and as he hitches up (if he has to) and passes the football. While in his drop, his shoulders should be slightly open to the line of scrimmage, which will allow him to see the entire field. His back should be fairly erect and he is *sitting down* more than he is leaning over at the waist. In addition, he will have his elbows in and close to the body, but not touching. The top end of the ball should be just about level with the top of the sternum, and held closely to his chest. The ball should be carried smoothly, with very little motion away from the center of his body. He should keep his chin close to his forward (left) shoulder to read his backside (Figures 1-1 and 1-2).

Figure 1-1. Example of a quarterback being compact.

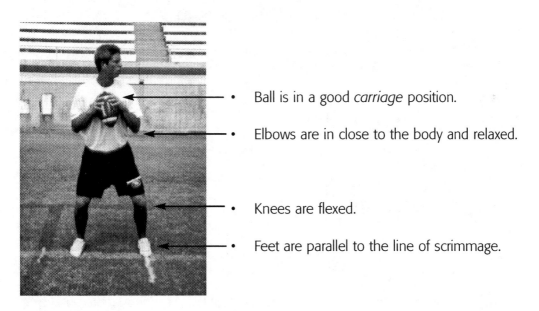

- Ball is in a good *carriage* position.

- Elbows are in close to the body and relaxed.

- Knees are flexed.

- Feet are parallel to the line of scrimmage.

Figure 1-2. Example of a quarterback being compact.

- The quarterback is ready to throw the football from a compact position.

- Just before making the throw, his front shoulder is pointed in the direction he wants the ball to go to.

- The ball is in a good *carriage* position.

- His elbows are in a comfortable, relaxed position, and close to his body.

- His knees are slightly bent, allowing him better leverage as he steps into the throw.

- His feet aren't too far apart, allowing him to step into the throw, and get good velocity and greater control on the football.

3/5/7-quick: Quick refers to the length of the quarterback's strides when dropping back to throw a pass. The quarterback should shorten his strides slightly and move his feet a little quicker to get the route to time out properly. When the quarterback uses these *quick* drops, he needs to realize timing is more important than depth.

3/5/7-big: Big tells the quarterback to lengthen his strides slightly when dropping back to throw a pass. The quarterback should not turn his shoulders away from the backside when lengthening his strides. He will slightly slow down the movement of his feet when he lengthens is strides which will allow him to throw the pass on time.

Hold: This tells the quarterback to hold the ball a fraction of a second when he hits the end of his drop. This action is designed to allow the receiver to finish his route and enable the quarterback to deliver the ball on time.

Hitch: This involves the action that occurs when the quarterback resets his back foot to throw. He should always hitch with his back foot to prevent overstriding.

Hitching-up: This refers to when the quarterback resets his back foot and then hitches forward in six-inch increments to allow the routes to develop, or to go through his check downs.

Roll-step: This occurs when the quarterback steps to the target-side with his plant foot, then steps toward the target with his lead step. He does this to get the ball to *tail-off* in the same direction as the receiver is headed (Figures 1-3 and 1-4).

Figure 1-3. Example of a roll-step

- This is a good example of a roll-step to the left side to throw an out route to the outside receiver.

- This figure shows the quarterback preparing to throw to an outside receiver on his backside to the left. He will then pick up his front foot (target-step) and step towards the point where the ball and receiver will meet on the left.

Figure 1-4. Example of a roll-step

- This is a good example of a roll-step to the right side in order to throw an out route to the outside receiver on the quarterback's front side on the right. He will then pick up his front foot (target-step) and step towards the point where the ball and receiver will meet on the right.

The Quarterback Stance

The quarterback's stance is a critical element in playing the position. It is important that the quarterback develop a comfortable and efficient stance to be able to execute all the movement necessary once the ball is snapped.

The proper stance allows the quarterback to move in any direction necessary due to the different types of action in any offense. For example, the footwork on an outside-stretch play is very different from the footwork on a dive play or a dropback pass. The quarterback also has to be able to mesh with the running back at several different places in the backfield, which include points to the left and right of the quarterback.

Upon exiting the huddle, the quarterback should get under the center as quickly as possible, before he starts his pre-snap read. This will force the defense to do any shifting or stemming at this point. Be sure to have both hands under the center. Usually the defense won't do anything until the quarterback is under the center because they know nothing can happen until the quarterback is ready to receive the ball (Figure 1-5).

It is also important that the entire offense get to the line quickly to give the quarterback time to see how the defense is setting up. The wide receivers should sprint to the line of scrimmage so the quarterback can get an idea of how the secondary is going to line up. Remember, unless you are at the NFL or elite college level, it's hard for the secondary to hide their coverage because they are usually out of position and unable to cover their area or man very well. This is especially true when defending the quick passing game. It should also be noted that many times offenses get delay of game penalties when a quarterback has to audible. This is usually due to the fact that he has no time once he gets set under center, because he has wasted time getting to the line of scrimmage, instead of using his time wisely at the line of scrimmage.

Figure 1-5. This is a good example of a quarterback stance behind the center.

The legs should be flexed comfortably with the shoulders square to the line of scrimmage. The quarterback should remain as tall as the center will permit, keeping his back straight and his head up checking the defenders. He should bend at the knees rather than the torso. This allows the quarterback a better line of vision when scanning the defense while under the center. Many quarterbacks crouch behind the center and are so low to the ground that they can't see the defense very well. This type of positioning doesn't allow the quarterback to be very efficient mechanically dropping back, or finding a good mesh with the running back.

Once the quarterback is at the line of scrimmage, his hands should be under the center's crotch, *knuckle deep*, spread apart to an angle of 90 degrees, with the thumbs together — letting the snapper know exactly where to place the ball (Figure 1-6). A key point here is that often when the quarterback receives the ball from center, he will automatically pull his wrists apart during the exchange. Even alerting the quarterback to this critical mistake will not take care of the problem. Instead, you will see the ball rolling up the forearm of the quarterback.

Figure 1-6. A quarterback with the correct hand positioning behind the center

- Elbows are slightly bent.

- Thumbs are together.

- Hands are spread apart to 90 degrees.

By having the quarterback keep his thumbs together, the hands usually won't come apart during the exchange. Instead, the left hand (in a right handed quarterback) will automatically wrap around the ball at the exchange. Remember, if you don't catch the problem right away and correct it, you are just getting repetitions doing something incorrect. If the quarterback is dropping or bobbling the snap, you must change what he is doing with his hands right away, and then rep it so that his muscle memory is retrained.

At this point the quarterback is set behind the center in a comfortable, efficient position, he must scan the defensive front, checking the alignment of the backers and getting a read on the secondary coverage. This will give him an idea of what the defense might be trying to do. He can then make any necessary adjustments.

Quarterbacks can somewhat control what the defense does before the snap by learning to vary the snap count on every play. The defense will have problems timing their shifts due to the fact that they can't really anticipate when the quarterback is going to start the play. This is something that should be worked on everyday. Just before the snap, the quarterback should have his head up and looking down field every time.

Summary of the Quarterback Stance

- Get under the center as quickly has possible.
- Have both hands under the center immediately.
- The entire offense should be at line of scrimmage a quickly as possible.
- The legs should be flexed comfortably.
- Remain as tall as possible while under the center.
- Bend at the knees rather than the torso.
- The hands should be spread to ninety-degrees.
- Keep the thumbs together.
- Scan the defense the same way every time.
- Always vary the snap count.

The Punch-Step

In separating from the center at the snap, the quarterback should ride the center forward with his hands and arms only. As the exchange is affected, he should take a short (six inches maximum) backward step with his left (punch-step) foot and pivot the foot slightly inward. This *punch-step* should be taken very quickly at the same time the quarterback is receiving the ball from center. This takes no more time than it would if the quarterback had his feet staggered, because he is taking the step as he is receiving the ball from the center (Figure 1-7).

The punch-step will help the quarterback disengage from the center and obtain the proper depth in his drop, while keeping his shoulders square to the line of scrimmage during the initial phase of the dropback. It will also prevent the quarterback from false stepping into the center during the exchange. Many NFL quarterbacks use this separation step and you have probably never even noticed it. It happens so quickly you might miss it all together if you weren't looking for it.

Figure 1-7. This is an example of a quarterback utilizing the punch-step

• The punch-step is taken no more than six inches and slightly pigeon-toed.

Another safety component of the punch-step is that it forces the quarterback's right hand to ride forward with the center during the exchange, which will guard against fumbled snaps. If the quarterback pulls out or backs out too early in the exchange, he is not able to secure the ball initially. You will see him adjusting the ball or bobbling the ball as he separates from the center, or dropping the ball all together. The sooner the quarterback can grip the ball in the proper manner, the better opportunity he has to hand the ball off, or drop back and throw an accurate pass (Figure 1-8).

Figure 1-8. One quarterback snapping the ball to the other quarterback

• The quarterback kneeling represents the center. His left hand represents the center's crotch. The hand should stay firm throughout the entire snap process. The snap should also be very firm and quick. Because the quarterback is primarily focused on his read or finding the mesh with the running back, he usually has no idea what is going awry with the center exchange. This is why the punch-step is so important to the quarterback's basic mechanics, and why a balanced stance in conjunction with the use of the punch-step is preferred over a staggered stance.

Summary of the Punch-Step

- Allows the quarterback to ride the center forward during exchange with throwing hand.
- Helps prevent false-steps.
- Allows the quarterback to get deeper in his drop.
- Takes a short step backward with his left foot (for a right-handed quarterback) during the exchange.
- Do not allow your hands to separate when receiving snap from center.

DRILL #1: THE PUNCH-STEP DRILL

Objective: To teach the quarterback the proper technique required to perform the punch-step properly.

Equipment Needed: One football and football cleats

Description: The coach will kneel down on one knee and hold his left hand at the same height the center's crotch would be. The quarterback should bend at the knees and sit high so he can scan the defense. He will go through his cadence and the coach will snap the ball to the quarterback with significant force to simulate the center exchange. The quarterback will take the punch-step as he is receiving the ball from the coach. There should be little retreat from the throwing shoulder during the point of exchange.

Coaching Points:

- The coach should make sure the quarterback does not pull out early.
- The punch-step should be exactly the same on every snap (with regard to the dropback-passing game).
- The coach should make sure the quarterback's hands do *not* come apart as he is receiving the ball from the center.
- The coach should make sure the quarterback moves his feet before his upper body.
- The quarterback should take at least a dozen reps each day.

Skill Simulated: Taking a precise punch-step during the quarterback-center exchange without pulling away from the center until the ball is secured.

DRILL #2: THE QUARTERBACK-CENTER EXCHANGE DRILL

Objective: To teach the quarterback the patience and the mechanics necessary to receive the ball from the center in a consistent and efficient manner.

Equipment Needed: One football and football cleats

Description: The quarterback should line up behind the center with his feet inside the snapper's heels and with his toes pointed slightly pigeon-toed (this prevents false stepping). His weight should be over the balls of his feet just enough to give him a comfortable, balanced feeling. He should bend at the knees and sit high so he can scan the defense. The coach should be low enough to view the point where the ball meets the quarterback's hands.

Coaching Points:

- This drill should always be done with a center.
- The coach should make sure the quarterback does not pull out early.
- The punch-step should be exactly the same on every snap (with regard to the dropback-passing game).
- Every hand off, play action, and dropback should be incorporated into this drill.
- The coach should make sure the quarterback's hands do not come apart as he is receiving the ball from the center.
- The quarterback should take at least a dozen reps each day.
- Usually quarterbacks will take the snap from the center by moving their upper body backwards first, which causes them to pull their hands out too soon. In reality, they should move their feet first and make sure the secure the ball by letting their upper body lag behind their feet a fraction of a minute.
- The coach should make sure the quarterback moves his feet before his upper body.

Skill Simulated: The quarterback-center exchange.

The Dropback

The first full step away from the center should be a long stride with the right foot and should also be very clean. This should be followed up with progressively shorter steps. As a general rule, the first two-thirds of the drop should be made up of fairly long strides, with the last third of the drop being composed of shorter, control-type steps. The feet should not come up off the ground much at all. They should almost skim the surface during the dropback.

The quarterback should have his shoulders slightly open to the line of scrimmage during his drop, which will put him in a position to see the entire field. Ideally, his drop will look the same to the defense, regardless of which side of the field he is reading. This is extremely important and cannot be stressed enough. This shoulder positioning during the quarterback's drop allows him to be cognizant of what is going on as far as blitzes and receiver play are concerned on the backside. In addition, the quarterback will have his feet in a better position to throw to the backside at anytime during his drop, which will measurably add to the accuracy of the pass thrown to that side (Figure 1-9).

Figure 1-9. A quarterback dropping back with his shoulders slightly open to the line of scrimmage

- Eyes are focused downfield.

- Ball carriage is good here.

- Shoulders are slightly open to line of scrimmage.

- Back is fairly erect.

- Good, flexed knees

- Feet should almost be parallel to line of scrimmage.

A three-step drop will take the quarterback about four to four and a half yards from the line of scrimmage. The five-step drop will take him from seven to seven and a half yards back, and the seven-step drop will take him about nine yards back (Figure 1-10).

During the dropback, the quarterback must go through his progressions so that when he hits the last step in his drop, he is knows where he will be throwing the football. We want very little or no hesitation by the quarterback.

It is important to remember that adjustments may be needed to maximize the quarterback's and receiver's efficiency. For example, in one offense, the quarterback may use a *7-big with a hitch step* on an 18-yard comeback route run by the wide receiver. If, however, the quarterback is late in his delivery, it may become necessary to change his drop to a 7-quick with a hitch step to time out the pattern.

As the quarterback comes to the end of his drop, he must execute the most critical elements of the pass: the front-shoulder drop, the back-plant step, the hitch step, the target-step, and the concluding follow-through.

Figure 1-10. These are dropback lines with depth markers. The quarterback is carrying the ball a bit too low, but he is staying compact and has excellent body position.

- Ideally, the top of the ball should be here. Young quarterbacks sometimes let the football get low on them as they hitch-up in their drop. You need to guard against this.

- This is a near perfect drop. The quarterback takes a 7-quick with a hitch drop and hits right at 8-yards.

Summary of the Dropback

- First full step should be a long stride.
- First two-thirds of the drop should be fairly long strides, with the last third being composed of shorter, control-type steps.
- The feet should stay close to the ground at all times.
- Shoulders should be slightly open to line of scrimmage during the entire drop.
- During the dropback, the quarterback must go through his progressions so that when he hits the last step in his drop, he is knows where he will be throwing the football.

DRILL #3: THE DROP-AT-DEPTH DRILL

Objective: To teach the quarterback what it feels like to drop back to the proper depth with balance, and with good body position, throwing to the appropriate receiver with good mechanics.

Equipment Needed: One football, football cleats, and a lined field with depth lines (Figure 1-11)

Description: The quarterback should line up behind the center (if there is no center, he should line up exactly one-yard behind the line of scrimmage. A receiver will stand where he would receive the pass if he were running the regular route. Start with short passes to the quarterback's backside and go through each specific route several times.

Coaching Points:

- The quarterback should always get to the proper depth on each drop within two inches (with the one exception of the 5-big with a hitch drop, which can be between seven and seven and a half yards in depth).
- The quarterback will drop back with the ball in good carriage position.
- The quarterback will have his shoulders slightly open to the line of scrimmage on all drops, regardless of which side he is throwing to.
- The quarterback will wait until the end of his drop before he points his shoulders to his target.
- Have the quarterback take his *no-hitch* drops before he takes his *hitch-step* drops.
- The quarterback will take the proper plant-step (perpendicular to his target) during each throw.
- The quarterback will throw each pass with the proper velocity in relation to the specific pass route being practiced.

Skill Simulated: Taking a precise, balanced drop with excellent mechanics and throwing each route in the entire offense perfectly.

Figure 1-11. This is an example of how to set up the *drop-at-depth lines*. You will get a lot of use out of this drill. It is an excellent way to teach the quarterback the precise depth he needs to be at during each throw.

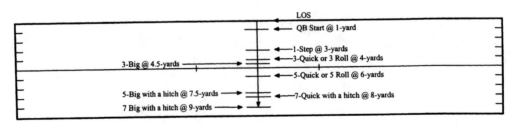

Quarterback Drops and Distances
(Measured from the line of scrimmage)

1-step: The quarterback drops back about three yards. Bubble screens (wide routes), quick-swing routes, and play-action quick routes. Also, fade routes from the five-yard line (Figures 1-12 and 1-13).

3-quick: The quarterback drops back about four yards. Hot routes, hitch routes, slant routes, and red-zone fade routes (Figure 1-14).

3-roll: The quarterback drops back about four yards. Quick-out routes run by the outside receiver (Figure 1-15).

3-big: The quarterback drops back about four and a half yards. Slant routes (Figure 1-16).

3-big, hold: The quarterback drops back about four and a half yards. Stick routes, middle routes, some slant routes and open-field fade routes (Figure 1-17).

5-quick: The quarterback drops about six yards. Skinny posts, drags, and flat routes (Figure 1-18).

5-roll: The quarterback drops about six yards. 12-yard speed-outs run by the outside receiver (Figure 1-19).

5-big, hold: The quarterback drops about seven yards. Swing routes, inside-corner routes, and drag routes (Figure 1-20).

5-big with a hitch-step: The quarterback drops about seven to seven and a half yards. Curl, square in, and go routes (Figure 1-21).

7-quick with a hitch-step: The quarterback drops about eight yards. Dig routes, smash routes, and corner routes inside the red zone (Figure 1-22).

7-big with a hitch-step: The quarterback drops about nine yards. Counter routes, post-corners routes, and comeback routes run by the outside receiver (Figure 1-23).

Figure 1-12. The quarterback drops about three yards from the line of scrimmage. Used on bubble screens (wide-routes), and quick-swing routes.

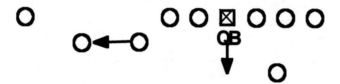

Figure 1-13. The quarterback drops about three yards from the line of scrimmage. NOTE: Both these routes are 4 throws (see Chapter 2 for throw descriptions).

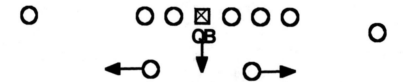

Figure 1-14. The quarterback drops about four yards from the line of scrimmage. Used on hot routes, hitch routes, and redzone fades.

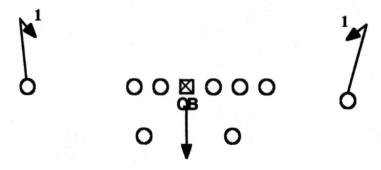

Figure 1-15. The quarterback drops about four yards from the line of scrimmage, allowing on quick throws to the wide receiver. Once the quarterback gets a pre-snap read, he should pick a side and stay with it, going from his primary receiver to his outlet. NOTE: Both the quick-hitch and quick-out routes are 1 throws.

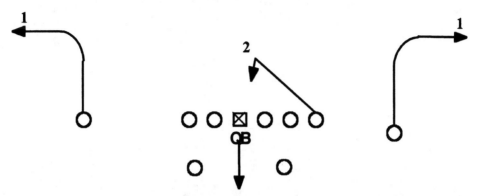

Figure 1-16. The quarterback will get back to about four and a half yards in depth. Use on quick slants run by the wide receivers. (Pick a side and stay with it.)

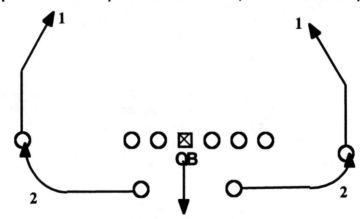

Figure 1-17. The quarterback will get back to about four and a half yards in depth stick routes run by the inside receivers. NOTE: Both the stick route and the slant routes are 1 throws.

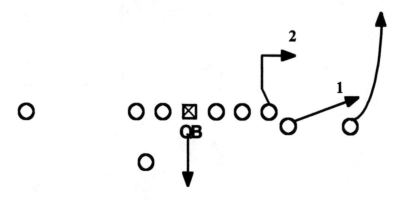

Figure 1-18. Used on 12-yard quick-seam posts by the wide receiver. The quarterback drops about six yards from the line of scrimmage, avoiding any kind of gather step. He should pick a side and stay with it, going from his primary receiver to his outlet.

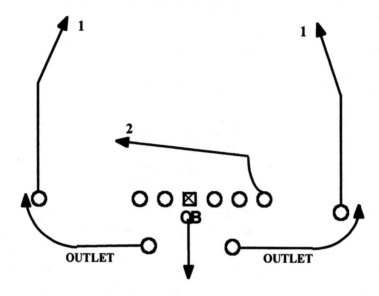

Figure 1-19. Used on 12-yard speed outs by the wide receiver. The quarterback will get back to about six yards from the line of scrimmage, allowing him to cheat in order to hit the wide receiver quickly. Once the quarterback gets a pre-snap read, he should pick a side and stay with it, going through his progressions.
NOTE: Both the post route and the sideline routes are 1 throws.

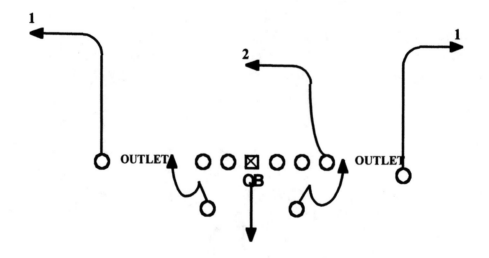

Figure 1-20. The quarterback drops about seven yards from the line of scrimmage. Used on corner routes run by the inside receivers and swing routes coming out of the back field.

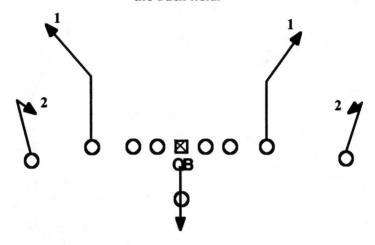

Figure 1-21. Used on 12-yard curls by the wide receivers. The quarterback drops about seven and a half yards from the line of scrimmage. He always hitches with the back foot to prevent overstriding. NOTE: The hitch and curl routes are 1 throws; the corners are 2 throws; and the swing routes are 4 throws.

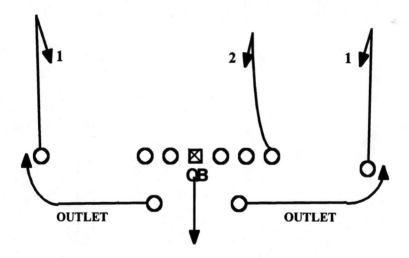

Figure 1-22. Used on 16-yard dig routes by the wide receivers. The quarterback drops to about eight yards from the line of scrimmage, and always hitches with the back foot to help prevent overstriding.

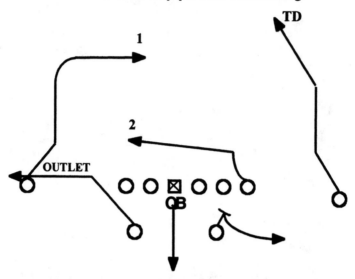

Figure 1-23. Used on 18-yard comeback routes and deep post-corner routes by wide receivers. The quarterback drops nine yards from the line of scrimmage, always hitches with the back foot to help prevent overstriding. NOTE: The dig route is a 1 throw, the post route is a 3 throw if it is thrown over the safety – it is a 1 throw if it is a single coverage timing throw. The drag is a 4 throw. The corner routes are usually 2 throws as is the post route run by the tight end.

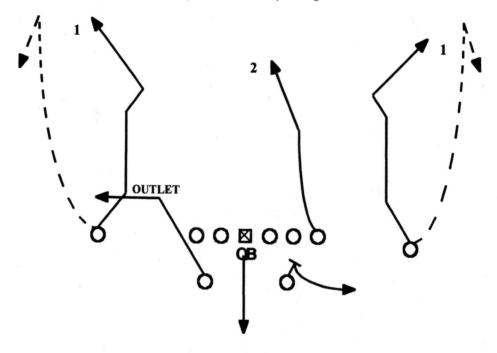

The Ball Carriage

As the quarterback drops back, he will have the ball chest high with the points of the ball vertical. He will have his elbows in and close to his body but not touching. The top end of the ball should be just about level with the top of his sternum. The ball should be carried smoothly, with very little motion away from the center of his body. He should keep his chin close to his forward (left) shoulder to read his backside. The grip of the throwing hand should be on the laces as it would be if the quarterback were throwing a pass. The off hand will cover the other side of the football and there should be some pressure applied from this offside. The grip should be firm but not to the point where he is squeezing the ball tightly. It should be done in a comfortable, secure manner. Remember, there should be very little movement of the ball during the dropback (Figure 1-24).

Figure 1-24. Examples of quarterbacks with good ball carriage.

Summary of the Ball Carriage

- The ball should be chest high with the points of the ball vertical.
- The top end of the ball should be level with the top of the sternum.
- The football should be carried smoothly with minimal motion away from the body.
- The chin should be kept close to the forward (left) shoulder.
- The quarterback should have a firm but relaxed grip.
- It should be comfortable and smooth during the dropback.

DRILL #4: THE BALL CARRIAGE

Objective: To teach the quarterback how to carry the football during the dropback and during any movement in the pocket.

Equipment Needed: One football and football cleats

Description: The quarterback will start his drop. The coach, standing in front of the quarterback, will point in the direction he wants the quarterback to move (right, left, backward, and forward). The quarterback will run the drill in a controlled pace, making sure that the ball stays in a good position with very little movement.

Coaching Points:

- The quarterback will drop back with the ball in good carriage position.
- The quarterback will have his shoulders slightly open to the line of scrimmage on all drops.
- The quarterback will exercise excellent technique during each repetition.
- The quarterback will be smooth in and out of his breaks.
- The quarterback will react to the signal and not guess which way to break.

Skill Simulated: Taking a balanced drop with excellent mechanics and securing the ball in a comfortable, efficient manner (Figure 1-25).

Figure 1-25.

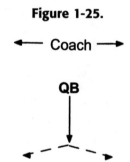

The Front-Shoulder Drop

As the quarterback nears the end of his drop, he must take shorter steps and initiate either a *no-hitch throw*, or use a *hitch-step* to reset his feet before he throws the football. You want him to drop is front shoulder slightly to stabilize himself and then take a little bounce forward as he transfers his weight from back to front..

If the quarterback throws off his back foot without using a front-shoulder drop to stabilize his shoulders, the ball will sail over the receiver's head. If he locks his knees because his feet are too far apart before he throws, he'll usually throw the ball into the ground.

The goal of the front-shoulder drop is to have the quarterback's shoulders level in relation to the horizon so that he can throw an accurate pass with the proper velocity or touch (Figure 1-26).

Figure 1-26.

- Excellent front shoulder drop to level the shoulders just before and during the throw.

- The top of the football should be here – he is carrying it a little low.

- He has good depth in his five-step drop. Before he hitches up, his plant foot should be between seven and seven and a half yards from the line of scrimmage.

Summary of the Front-Shoulder Drop

- The quarterback should take shorter steps near the end of his drop.
- The quarterback should drop his front shoulder slightly to stabilize and level the shoulders for the throw.
- The quarterback should make sure his shoulders are level during the throw (except on deep throws).

The Plant-Step

One of the most critical components of the drop is the establishment of a solid, comfortable plant foot and the possible resetting (*hitch*) of that foot into the best throwing position. The quarterback's back foot must always be planted (with most of the weight on the ball of the foot so the heal is slightly off the ground) perpendicular to the target, putting him in the best position to make the throw. Quarterbacks often have difficulty throwing to their backside because they have placed their back foot perpendicular to the middle of the field rather than to their backside target, thereby forcing them to throw across their body (Figure 1-27).

Figure 1-27.

• This is an example of the quarterback repositioning his plant-foot in order to get it perpendicular to his target.

Summary of the Plant-Step

- The plant-step should be placed perpendicular to the target.
- Most of the quarterback's weight should be on the inside ball of the foot.

DRILL #5: THE PITCHER'S PICKOFF DRILL

Objective: To teach the quarterback to reposition his plant foot perpendicular to his target.

Equipment Needed: One football and football cleats

Description: The quarterback will start in his compact position at the end of his drop with his feet in good, ready position. The coach (or another player) will stand at various points downfield where receivers would normally catch the pass. The quarterback will then reposition his back foot perpendicular to his target, then step forward with his target step and throw the pass, much like a pitcher would when trying to pick off a man on base.

Coaching Points:

- The quarterback will stand where he would be at the end of his drop.
- The quarterback will be in his ready compact position.
- The quarterback will have his shoulders slightly open to the line of scrimmage on all drops.
- The quarterback will exercise excellent technique during each repetition.
- The quarterback will reposition his back foot *before* he steps to the target.

Skill Simulated: Repositioning the back foot so it is perpendicular to the target before the throw.

The Target-Step

With his body compact, a bend in his knees, and his feet about 12-inches apart, the quarterback is in the best position to throw the football quickly with velocity and accuracy, much like a baseball pitcher from a stretch position. It is important for the quarterback to point the inside portion of his lead foot toward the target receiver, or where the receiver will be when he catches the pass. The quarterback does not have to take an extremely long stride, since this might cause him to lock out his knee and throw the ball short into the ground. Furthermore, if done over a period of time, this may cause him pain and create arm trouble.

As the quarterback lands on his stride foot (heel to toe), his front knee should be slightly flexed with his foot pointed toward where the target and the ball will meet. If he lands toe first, his knee will most likely lock out, and he could wind up throwing the ball into the ground.

Anytime the quarterback has to move up into the pocket to find an outlet receiver, he should hitch-step forward, keeping his feet no more than 18-inches apart. When hitching up in the pocket, he should always bring his back foot forward first, preventing overstriding.

Figure 1-28. This is an example of both the plant-step (back foot) and the target-step. The plant-step is perpendicular to the target, while the target-step is pointed towards where the ball and target will meet.

- His hips are squared to the target.

- He has an excellent bend in his front knee.

- His target foot is pointed to where the ball and target will meet.

- His plant-step is perpendicular to his target.

Summary of the Target-Step

- The quarterback's body should be compact.

- The quarterback should have a bend in the knees.

- The quarterback should point the inside portion of his lead foot toward where the ball needs to go.

- The quarterback should not overstride.

- The quarterback should land on his stride foot (target-step), heel to toe.

- If the quarterback has to move up in the pocket, he should hitch-up *back foot first* to prevent overstriding.

DRILL #6: THE THROWING-THE-DRAG-ROUTE DRILL

Objective: To teach the quarterback to step in the direction of where his target receiver will be when he is catching the pass.

Equipment Needed: One football and football cleats

Description: The quarterback will start in his compact position at the end of his drop with his feet in good, ready position. The coach (or another player) will jog across at about five yards past the line of scrimmage. The quarterback will then step towards where the ball and target will meet with his target-step as he is throwing the pass.

Coaching Points:

- The quarterback will stand where he would be at the end of his drop, or he can take his full drop.

- The quarterback will stay compact.

- The quarterback will have his shoulders slightly open to the line of scrimmage on all drops.

- The quarterback will exercise excellent technique during each repetition. He will reposition his back foot before he throws to his target receiver.

- The quarterback will step towards where the ball and target will meet at the point of the reception.

- Make sure the quarterback does not throw behind the receiver as he is moving across his vision.

Skill Simulated: Stepping towards where the quarterback wants the pass to go rather than to where the target is at the time of the throw. You do not want the quarterback throwing behind the receiver (Figure 1-29).

Figure 1-29.

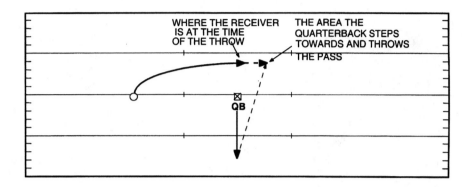

The No-Hitch Throw

In every passing offense, the quarterback will sometimes not use a hitch-step (reset) before he throws the pass. For example, in every quick pass, a hitch-step isn't necessary because it will adversely affect the timing of the throw, and the route will break open before the quarterback is able to throw the football. Other five-step pass routes also necessitate (because of timing requirements) the ball be thrown without using a hitch-step. You should teach the quarterbacks the proper mechanics to throw without using a hitch first, because it works out better down the road in the teaching progression.

As the quarterback takes his last crossover step (the second step in a three-step drop) his third step (plant-step) will hit the ground at approximately six to eight inches past his second step. That is to say his feet will only be six to eight inches apart as he steps forward with his target-step to throw the ball. At the same time, he will drop his front shoulder to stabilize his shoulders to a level position for the throw (Figure 1-30). It is imperative that the quarterback drop back in a controlled manner in the quick-passing game to throw an accurate and consistent pass with the proper velocity.

In a three-step drop, the quarterback will gain depth with his first step, then use a controlled crossover step, then a short plant-step. This should put him four to four and a half yards from the line of scrimmage just before the throw (Figure 1-31).

In a five-step, no-hitch drop, the quarterback will gain depth with his first step, then take short, quick steps for the remainder of his drop. In this case, timing is more important than depth. The quarterback should be at a depth of six yards from the line of scrimmage just before the throw. This type of throw requires the ball be about half way to the target before the receiver looks back for the ball.

Figure 1-30.

• This is where the plant-step should go when the quarterback is using a *no-hitch* type drop. At the same time, he should drop his front shoulder to stabilize his shoulders to a level throwing position.

Figure 1-31. This is an example of the footwork in a no-hitch throw. The quarterback drops back to four and a half yards. His plant-step is shorter at this point because he won't be using a hitch-step. He needs to do this so he can step into the throw without his feet being too far apart, which would cause his front knee to lock out, and the ball to go into the ground, short of the target.

• The feet are close together and the quarterback begins to step toward the receiver.

• The center of gravity is in front of the quarterback's plant step.

• His depth is at four and a half yards.

Summary of the No-Hitch Throw

- No-hitch throws are used in the quick-passing game as well and in some five-step drops.

- This should be taught early in the quarterback's development.

- During the quarterback's last crossover step, the plant-step is placed within eight inches of the front foot.

- As the crossover step is initiated, the quarterback should drop his front shoulder to stabilize his shoulders to a level position for the throw.

DRILL #7: THROWING-WITHOUT-A- HITCH DRILL

Objective: To teach the quarterback the proper technique of throwing an accurate pass with the proper velocity without using a hitch-step. This type of drop is used primarily for three-step drops (quick-passing game), as well as some five-step drops.

Equipment Needed: One football per quarterback, football cleats, and a lined field

Description: The coach will call a pass route that requires the quarterback to use a *no-hitch drop*. The quarterback will take the appropriate drop and throw the pass to the target receiver.

Coaching Points:

- As the quarterback starts to take his last crossover step, he should drop his front shoulder to initiate the transfer of weight from moving back away from the line of scrimmage to moving forward towards the intended target.

- The quarterback will take a short balance step after his last crossover step to prevent his feet from being too far apart before the throw.

- The last balance step should have the quarterback's feet no wider than shoulder-width apart.

- The quarterback will then step towards the target receiver and deliver the football with the proper follow-through.

Skill Simulated: Throwing all the quick-game passes as well as selected five-step passes. This is essential in providing the quarterback the fundamentals for efficient passing in this phase of the game (Figure 1-32).

Figure 1-32.

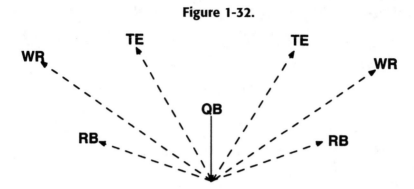

The Hitch-Step Throw

The most common 5, 7, and shotgun-type throws are the *hitch-step* throws. The hitch-step involves the action that occurs when the quarterback resets his back foot to throw. He will hit his last step (his feet will be about three-feet apart at this time) and then hitch-up with the back foot so that his feet come within inches of each other. Then he will push off this back foot as he steps towards his target receiver with his front foot, and transfer his weight forward, smoothly and effectively (Figures 1-33, a and b).

This hitch-step does two things: first, it allows the throw to time-out better with the receiver; and two, this extra step towards the target will allow the quarterback to drive himself forward to get all of his weight (the hips and shoulders) over his front foot as he throws the football. This will help him to throw a more accurate pass, with the potential for maximum velocity and the greatest control.

Most of the quarterback's power and inertia will come from his legs, hips, torso, and shoulders, which will transfer to the ball as it is released. All these body movements need to be synchronized to get the maximum control and velocity out of the throw. The quarterback needs to learn how to put his body in the best position to throw the ball further with superior accuracy and control.

Figure 1-33a.

- This is approximately where the quarterback will land on his next step *before* he hitches up to throw the pass.

Figure 1-33b. In this example, the QB has just hit the last step in his drop. He has to hitch-up before he throws the pass.

- The QB's feet are too far apart at this point to throw an accurate pass. He will hitch-up to reset his feet so they are closer together before he steps into the throw.

Summary of the Hitch-Step Throw

- It is the most common of all the throws.
- When the quarterback hits his last step, his feet will be too far apart to throw a well-controlled pass.
- The quarterback will then hitch-up with the back foot before stepping into the throw.
- It allows the throw to time-out better.
- It allows an accurate pass with good velocity.

DRILL #8: THE HITCH-ISOLATION DRILL

Objective: To teach the quarterback how to throw a pass using a hitch-step in his drop.

Equipment Needed: One football and football cleats

Description: The quarterback will stand with his shoulders perpendicular to the line of scrimmage in a good *compact* position with his feet approximately three-feet apart and knees flexed. The quarterback will then initiate the last crossover step in his drop, and then hit the last step in his drop. At this point he will hitch-up by bringing his back foot within inches of his front foot, and step towards his target receiver with his target step as he throws the pass.

Coaching Points:

- The quarterback will maintain a compact body posture throughout the drill.
- The quarterback will drop his front shoulder to stabilize his shoulders into a level position at the time of the throw.
- The quarterback will make sure his plant-step is always perpendicular to his target.

- The quarterback will step towards the point where he wants the ball to travel with the inside portion of his target-step.
- The quarterback will follow through using excellent mechanics.

Skill Simulated: Throwing an excellent pass while using a hitch-step in the quarterback's drop (Figure 1-34).

Figure 1-34.

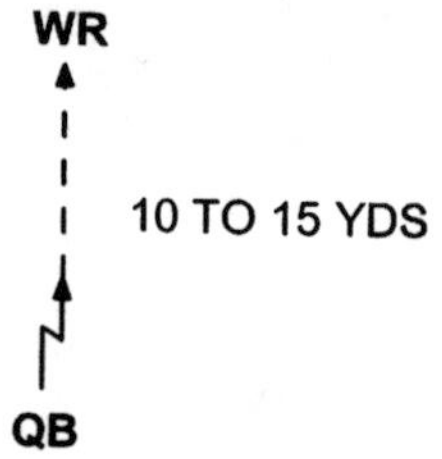

WR
▲
⋮
⋮
⋮   10 TO 15 YDS
⋮
▲
↱

QB

The Grip

The quarterback's grip on the football is very important and can often mean the difference between throwing a spiral or a wobbly pass. One of the most important things a quarterback should *not* do is to grip the football too tightly. When this happens, the pass thrown is usually not a spiral. So the quarterback's grip should be firm, but certainly not tight. There should also be a space between the ball and the palm of the hand (Figure 1-35).

Figure 1-35. This is a good example of the space between the palm of the hand and the football.

• This is where the space should be seen.

Obviously, the smaller the quarterback's hand is, the higher he will probably have to grip the ball. The fingers should be spread apart evenly across the ball and always on the laces. This will give the quarterback much more control of the rotation of the football.

The quarterback should experiment with different fundamentally sound grips until he finds one that works well for him. But he should remember that there should always be a space between the ball and his palm, he should grip the laces, and finally, his index finger will always be the last to leave the football. This causes a callous on the inside portion of his index finger after several weeks of throwing the football.

Summary of the Grip

- It controls the rotation of the football.
- The quarterback shouldn't grip the ball too tightly.
- The quarterback should have a space between the ball and the palm of his hand.

The Shoulder Spin

The shoulder spin is a technique that is used to increase the rotation-velocity of the football. A faster rotation-velocity will make the pass much easier for the receiver to catch, and the ball will cut through the air much more smoothly. A pass with a great deal of rotation-velocity will create a tight spiral that will be much more accurate in windy or rainy weather.

The quarterback should step into the throw with his front shoulder pointed in the direction he is throwing the pass. As he releases the football, he should spin his shoulders so that his back shoulder will be facing that same area once the ball is released. The quarterback must keep his shoulders level throughout the shoulder spin (except when throwing the deep ball).

Summary of the Shoulder Spin

- The quarterback steps into the throw with his front shoulder pointed in the direction he is throwing the pass.
- As he releases the football, the quarterback spins his shoulders so that his back shoulder will be facing that same area once the ball is released.
- The quarterback must keep his shoulders level throughout the shoulder spin (except when throwing the deep ball).

Figure 1-36.

- As the quarterback steps into the throw, his front shoulder is pointed in the direction he is throwing the pass.

- His shoulders are level and his front elbow is coming down through to his side.

- His front knee has a good bend in it, and he does not overstride.

Figure 1-37.

- Once the quarterback begins the throwing motion, his eyes stay locked on his target (never watch the football).

- The back shoulder is now pointing to where the pass and the target met.

- The throwing hand is now on his opposite hip.

- The plant foot comes to a point almost even with the target-step.

The Release

In his ready position, the quarterback should have his body under control, his feet about shoulder-width apart under his hips, his knees bent, and the ball held in both hands at chest level. As his lead foot is brought forward, the quarterback's support hand should gently push the ball back just before it comes off the ball completely. At this time, as the body moves forward, the hips and shoulders are level in relation to the ground. Then as the ball in the throwing hand comes back to a point behind the head, the non-passing elbow comes down and back across the left side of the body. The hips and shoulders start to open and the ball is released just after the hips and shoulders are parallel to the line of scrimmage.

The release is done with a smooth, synchronized action of the quarterback's feet, legs, trunk, hips, and throwing arm. It should be noted that the quarterback's index finger on his throwing hand is the dominant digit. It leaves the ball last as the quarterback's arm follows through toward the center of his body. The quarterback's throwing hand winds up with his palm facing the ground and his fingers pointing toward where the target and ball will meet (Figure 1-38). Quarterbacks who throw the ball a lot will get a callus on the inside edge of the tip of their index finger. This is produced by the friction of the ball against the last point of contact.

Figure 1-38.

- The ball has got a good trajectory – it is pointed up and slightly to the right.

- The eyes are focused on the target.

- The palm is facing the ground.

- The hips are square to the target.

- The front knee is slightly bent.

- The target-step is pointed where the ball is going.

Summary of the Release

- As the quarterback's lead foot is brought forward, his support hand should gently push the ball back just before it comes off the ball completely.
- The quarterback's hips and shoulders should be level in relation to the ground.
- The off elbow comes down across the body and the quarterback steps into the throw.
- The quarterback's index finger is the last digit to come off the ball.

DRILL #9: THROWING-ON-BOTH-KNEES RELEASE DRILL (3H)

Objective: To allow the quarterback's body to teach him good throwing motion.

Equipment Needed: One football

Description: This is an excellent way for the quarterback to learn how to throw a football using good throwing mechanics because he cannot compensate for bad throwing technique with his body. The quarterback will get on both knees and throw to a target no more than eight yards from him. He will continue to throw passes until he finds his proper throwing motion. This drill should be done every day so that he can train his muscle memory to throw in the proper and efficient manner on every pass.

Coaching Points:

- The quarterback will have a good grip on the football.
- The quarterback will continue to throw the football until he finds the best throwing motion, allowing him to throw consistent spirals that are accurate with good rotation.
- The quarterback will keep his body square to his target.
- The quarterback will follow through on all his throws.

Skill Simulated: Throwing a good pass using good throwing mechanics with shoulders level and hips squared-up to the target (Figure 1-39).

Figure 1-39.

- This is an example of a prepractice drill designed to teach the quarterback a good, fundamentally sound throwing motion. This is an excellent drill if your quarterback is having trouble discovering his proper throwing motion.

The Follow-Through

While the follow-through is an essential part of the quarterback's throwing action, this function has often been misinterpreted; once the ball leaves the quarterback's hand, he can do nothing more for the throw – the ball is gone.

However, the helpful feature of the follow-through is to give the quarterback and his coach a relatively good idea of what was done right and wrong in the throw. The coach can check all of the quarterback's key body areas (i.e., hand, wrist, elbow, arm, head, shoulders, hips, knees, feet, etc.) to make sure everything is where it ought to be. One other thing the coach or quarterback can look at is the flight of the ball. Any flaw in technique can show up in the flight of the ball. One very important thing the quarterback should always do is to watch the receiver (not the flight of the ball) until the football is caught. This will improve his accuracy in a very dramatic way, and in a short period of time.

As a rule, the quarterback's passing hand should flow toward the center of his body and wind up with his palm facing the ground and his fingers pointing toward where the target and the ball will meet. When all of his mechanics are executed correctly, the quarterback will deliver the ball with a tight spiral that achieves distance and accuracy without wasted motion or effort. It is much, much easier throwing the football using proper mechanics (Figure 1-40).

Figure 1-40.

- Eyes are focused on the target.

- His back shoulder is now pointing at the target.

- Good hand position on follow-through.

- He still has some bend in his front knee.

- His plant-step comes almost even with his target-step after the throw.

Summary of the Follow-Through

- Once the ball leaves the quarterback's hand, he can do nothing more to change the flight of the ball.
- The quarterback should always watch the receiver (not the flight of the ball) until the football is caught
- The quarterback's follow-through shows all key areas of the throw.

DRILL #10: THE FOLLOW-THROUGH DRILL

Objective: To teach the quarterback how to get his hips square to his target, and to rotate his shoulders when throwing a pass.

Equipment Needed: One football, football cleats, and a line.

Description: The quarterback will be approximately 10 to 15 yards from the target. He will be in a similar position to a pitcher about to pitch from the stretch position. He will be in a good *compact* position. His knees will be flexed, his back fairly erect, with the football in a good *carriage* position. His heels will be on the line, and his front shoulder will be pointed at the target. As the quarterback steps to the target, his target foot will cross the line (this will insure that his hips open up). As he releases the football, his throwing shoulder will end up pointing to the target.

Coaching Points:

- The quarterback will use proper throwing mechanics while passing the football.
- The quarterback will exaggerate the shoulder rotation and hold it until after the pass has been caught.
  - √ The quarterback will make sure his trail leg comes through and lands slightly in front of his target-step.
  - √ The quarterback should concentrate on the target – not the flight of the ball while it is in the air.

This drill should be done after the *Throwing-on-Both-Knees Release Drill* and after the quarterback has warmed up. It is desirable that the drill be done every day to make sure the quarterback has a habit of follow-through on all of his throws.

Skill Simulated: To consistently be able to get the quarterback's hips squared-up to the target on every throw and to be able to follow though properly to assure an accurate throw (Figures 1-41 and 1-42).

Figure 1-41. This is an example of the quarterback exaggerating his follow-through during the warm-up drill.

Figure 1-42.

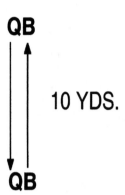

QB

10 YDS.

QB

Throwing the Deep Ball

Throwing the deep ball is a little different than throwing most passes in that the quarterback should tilt his shoulders upward as he steps into the throw. He also needs to concentrate on his follow-through on the throw (Figure 1-43).

Figure 1-43. The quarterback is ready to step into the throw once he has tilted his shoulders upward.

- The quarterback's forward shoulder is tilted upward.

- The quarterback has good ball carriage.

By tilting his shoulders upward as he steps into the throw, the nose of the ball will point upward naturally as the ball is released. When the quarterback exercises good mechanics, the ball will *turn over* as it approaches the target, which will lead to a good follow-throw on the throw.

One other important point to make here is that the quarterback should always keep his eyes on the target once he has released the ball. The brain will tell the hand what it has to do to get the ball to the target, so that if he misses that first throw, he will improve his accuracy on the next throw.

This is the same principal a baseball players uses as he runs around the bases. He will stagger or lengthen his strides as he is coming around the bases so that the appropriate foot hits the bag at the appropriate spot. It is not something he does consciously; the brain does it automatically. As the quarterback focuses on the target (instead of the flight of the ball) while the ball is in the air, a similar adjustment takes place so that the quarterback becomes more accurate with his throws almost immediately.

It is also important to realize that deep throws are timing passes. Many times, when a quarterback hesitates on this type of throw, the receiver outruns the pass. Similarly, the quarterback attempts to get too much on the throw (unconsciously realizing that at this point the target is out of his range) and the pass flutters as it travels though the air and ultimately falls short of the target.

Usually, the standard drop on a deep pass is 5-big with a hitch. However, many quarterbacks may be more comfortable with a 5-quick and a hitch drop. The quarterback (as well as the coach) can usually tell by the quarterback's third step in his drop if his intended target will be open. If this approach doesn't provide enough insight, another good rule is that if the receiver isn't even with the defender on the quarterback's fifth step in his drop, he won't be open when the ball gets there. He should then check-off to an underneath receiver by hitching up one more time and getting rid of the ball, or taking off on his own to get at least to the original line of scrimmage.

On fade routes (routes thrown in the red-zone) the drops are as follows: from the 15 to 20 yard line you should use a 3-big throw drop. From 6 to 15 yards, you should use a 3-quick and throw drop, and from the five-yard line you should use a 1-step and throw drop. These three-step drops also require that the quarterback pitch his shoulders upward as he is throwing the pass and use good mechanics for a good follow-through. In addition, the quarterback should pick a receiver on his pre-snap read and stick with him!

DRILL #11: THE DROP-IT-DOWN-THE-CHIMNEY DRILL

Objective: To practice the trajectory and necessary *turn over* for the deep ball.

Equipment Needed: Several footballs per quarterback, football cleats, a lined field, and one large garbage can.

Description: The coach should place a large garbage can at 44-yards downfield, several yards away from the sideline. The quarterback will take a 5-big with a hitch- step drop and throw the ball high enough so that in turns over and goes into the garbage can.

Coaching Points:

- The quarterback will take a 5-big with a hitch-step drop, and throw the ball (a 3 throw) to the garbage can.
- The quarterback will have his shoulder pointed slightly upward.
- The quarterback will use proper mechanics and emphasize his follow-through to get the ball to *turn over* and drop into the garbage can.
- The quarterback will throw the ball on time.

Skill Simulated: Throwing an accurate deep pass (a 3-type throw), which is a timing pass.

Note: This drill can also be used as a red-zone fade drill. Just place the can in the corner of the end zone to simulate the quick red-zone fade pass (Figure 1-44).

Figure 1-44.

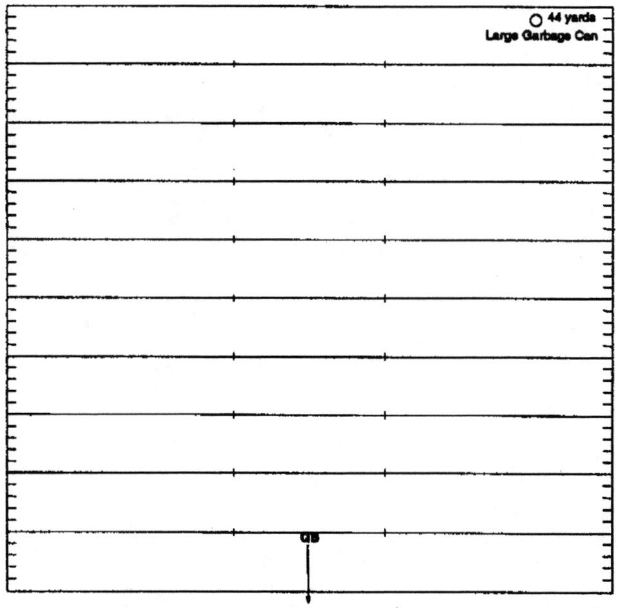

Summary of Throwing the Deep Ball

- The quarterback should tilt his shoulders upward as he steps into the throw.
- When the quarterback exercises good mechanics, the ball will turn over as it approaches the target, which will lead to a good follow-throw on the throw.
- The quarterback should always keep his eyes on the target once he has released the ball.
- Deep throws are timing passes.
- The standard drop on a deep pass is 5-big with a hitch-step drop.
- The red-zone fade routes can be anywhere from a 3-big throw to a 1-step throw depending on the distance from the end zone.

CHAPTER 2

The Different Types of Passes

Introduction

One of the very important things a quarterback can do to increase his completion percentage is to control the velocity, as well as the arc, of his passes. Young quarterbacks throw most of their passes too hard. One of the reasons for this is that they wait for their receiver to break open (instead of anticipating when he will break open), and then they have to force the ball because the defense is collapsing around the open receiver.

Receivers often drop passes because they are thrown too hard, are poorly placed, or are not thrown at the appropriate time. Receivers usually get the blame from the coaches, but it ends up on the quarterback's statistics, and hurts the efficiency of the offense, which can affect the outcome of the game. It would be in the quarterback's best interest to do what he can to increase the probability his passes will be caught.

Most quarterback coaches use a number system to describe to their quarterbacks what type of throws they should make. Quarterbacks will throw five basic types of passes at any given time. The passes are rated based on the velocity and the arc of the ball. A type-1 throw has the most velocity on it, but has little arc to it. A type-5 throw has the most touch on it as well as the most arc to it. It's important to remember that the longer the ball is in the air, the more of an opportunity the defense has to converge on it. The following are the five types of passes that are thrown.

The Type-1 Throw

This is the type of throw that has the most velocity on it. It is sometimes said that the quarterback has thrown a *rope* when he throws this type of pass. This type of pass is usually used when the receiver is running away from the quarterback, such as a deep-out route, or when the quarterback has to put the ball between defenders. Many times this throw will be used on 15- to 20-yard square-in routes, outside-curl routes, and skinny-post routes (Figure 2-1).

Type-1 Throws – Examples of Specific Routes: Out routes, comeback routes, some dig and square-in routes, as well outside-curl routes, and skinny-post routes.

Figure 2-1. The trajectory of a type-1 throw might look something like this from the side view. Notice there is very little arch. It has a lot of velocity on it and good rotation. The quarterback is usually throwing between defenders or to a receiver running a deep out or comeback route.

The Type-2 Throw

This type of throw is used when the quarterback needs to get the ball to the receiver right away, but still needs to put enough air under it to get it over linebackers or second-level defenders. An example would be a pass that has to travel over the linebacker, but still be able to get to the receiver before the safety coverage can converge on the throw. This is still a pass that has velocity on it but there is a little air under it (Figure 2-2).

Type-2 Throws – Examples of Specific Routes: Cover 2 fade routes, some dig routes, and corner routes.

Figure 2-2. The trajectory of a type-2 throw might look something like this from the side view. Because it most likely has to travel over defenders, the arch is greater, but it still needs good velocity and good ball rotation.

The Type-3 Throw

(See the section in Chapter 1 entitled *Throwing the Deep Ball* to utilize the specific technique of this throw.)

This type of pass is used primarily on go routes, fades, and some post and corner routes. On this type of pass, the quarterback will put the ball up and in front of the receiver. At this point, the receiver will accelerate to the ball and catch the football over his shoulder. The ball has a more pronounced trajectory from the throw (Figure 2-3).

Type-3 Throws – Examples of Specific Routes: Go routes and some deep play-action post routes.

Figure 2-3. The trajectory of a type-3 throw might look something like this from the side view. The ball is thrown out in front of the receiver with a greater arch as he runs away from coverage. As the receiver looks back for the pass, he will accelerate to the football.

The Type-4 Throw

This is a throw that many quarterbacks don't make, even though it is used when the intended receiver is close to the quarterback at the time of the throw. Usually, the receiver is catching the ball just past the line of scrimmage, underneath the linebacker coverage, such as on a drag route, or even a dump-off pass to the running back when he is just yards beyond the line of scrimmage.

Frequently, the quarterback throws this pass too hard and the receiver can't make the fine adjustments necessary for catching a pass at that speed. This type of pass needs to be thrown with less velocity on it so the receiver, running at a good rate of speed, can make the adjustments needed to catch the pass, secure the ball, then find the seam to run through. Because the throw is so short, the arch is much smaller. Often times the quarterback doesn't have to really step into the throw to get it to the receiver (Figure 2-4).

Type-4 Throws – Examples of Specific Routes: Drag routes and routes to running backs as they release over the middle.

Figure 2-4. The trajectory of a type-4 throw might look something like this from the side view. Because it is a shorter pass, the arch is much smaller, but the pass still has to have a lot of touch. You want good rotation on the ball and you want to place it just in front of the receiver about chest high so the receiver easily catches it.

The Type-5 Throw

This is the type of throw is used on screen passes. Usually, the ball must be thrown over a rusher to the intended receiver. You should try to get the quarterback to throw a tight spiral that can be caught with one hand by the receiver (even though you shouldn't ever teach your receiver to catch passes with one hand). This type of throw needs to be practiced by the quarterback to develop the proper technique so that he can get an accurate pass off with a good spiral, even thought he is throwing off balance. Because the quarterback is usually throwing over an oncoming rusher as well as for timing purposes, the arch on the trajectory is much more pronounced. The quarterback will almost jump vertically and slightly backwards as he throws this pass. He also has to attempt to exaggerate the overhand throws, with an excellent follow-throw to get a spiral with good rotation. You really don't want a pass that wobbles because it can be difficult to catch (Figure 2-5). It is also important to note the times when the quarterback will throw this pass with some velocity between defenders (something like a 4 throw) when it is necessary.

Type-5 Throws – Examples of Specific Routes: Some of the screen passes – especially to the inside oncoming rushers. You also want a lot of touch and good rotation on the ball, so that the receiver could almost catch the ball with one hand if he had to.

Figure 2-5. The trajectory of a type-5 throw might look something like this from the side view. You want the highest arch on the pass possible, as it may have to be thrown over.

Summary of the Different Types of Passes Thrown

- Many quarterbacks try to throw passes too hard.
- 1 throw – to throw between defenders.
- 2 throw – to throw over second-level defenders and in front of third- level defenders.
- 3 throw – throwing it out in front of receivers on deep passes.
- 4 throw – to throw to receivers close to the quarterback.
- 5 throws – some of the screen passes.

CHAPTER 3

Common Flaws in Quarterback Mechanics

Introduction

Many times when you're working with a new quarterback, your first concern should be with breaking his bad habits. You should start by explaining what the new technique can do for him and how the technique he's using is counter-productive to his goal of becoming a better quarterback. Quarterbacks usually make improvements immediately because they could feel and see the benefits of proper techniques and mechanics right away. The following lists of techniques sometimes taught to quarterbacks are fundamentally unsound and must be corrected.

Poor Hand Placement Under the Center

When you see the quarterback's hands come apart at the exchange so that the ball rolls up the quarterbacks arm, you've got a problem. Many times, the quarterback's hands are in a poor position from the start. When the ball is snapped, the quarterback's hands come apart just as the ball hits his hands. The ball squirts through his hands and starts to roll up his forearm. The quarterback finally gets a good grip on the football after his first or second step away from center. Sometimes, the ball is fumbled (Figure 3-1).

What the quarterback needs to do is make a deliberate effort to keep both of his thumbs together as he receives the ball from center. The throwing hand should always be on top with the thumbs together. The quarterback needs to be cognizant to make sure the bottom hand wraps around the football during the center exchange. Don't allow his hands to come apart during the exchange.

Figure 3-1. This is a common problem for quarterbacks – the hands coming apart during the center exchange.

- The quarterback's lower hand comes apart from the upper hand as the quarterback is receiving the snap from center.

Getting As Deep As You Can As Fast As You Can in Your Drop

This is very common, and although this practice is all but gone in the NFL, you will still see this at the high school level. Dropping back too fast in an uncontrolled manner is bad for several reasons.

First, it forces you to turn your shoulders away from the line of scrimmage while you are dropping back. You can't see your backside and you have to swing your body all the way around to throw to the backside. When you finally get to the end of your drop, you have only a short time to locate your read keys and find your receivers.

Second, when you are flying back in your drop, you have to make a violent effort to stop and get set to throw the football. Most likely, your shoulders are pitched back and are not level enough to throw and accurate pass. This will obviously have a negative effect with respect to proper throwing mechanics.

Finally, when you get to your drop-point, you have to wait for the receiver to break open. When you stay in one spot (even if you are keeping your feet moving) you tend to tense up and you are also the target for the rushers (Figure 3-2).

Figure 3-2. This is an example of a quarterback trying to get as deep as he can, as fast as he can, in his drop. He has to turn his shoulders away from the line of scrimmage to do this. He can't see what is happening on his backside. If he wanted to throw there, he wouldn't be able to see what was happening there until he got to the end of his drop.

- The quarterback can't see what is happening on his backside.

- His shoulders are turned away from the line of scrimmage.

- His hips are turned away from the line of scrimmage. It would take great effort to be able to square his hips to a backside target.

- His feet are turned completely away from the line of scrimmage. It would be very difficult to be able to get his plant-foot perpendicular to a backside target.

The best type of drop is one where the quarterback gets to a prescribed depth in a smooth and efficient manner. He should get rid of the ball the instant the receiver is breaking open, or he should hitch up in the pocket looking for the route to develop downfield. The quarterback should also be in a position to throw throughout his drop in case he has to throw hot or even throw the ball away. He should also drop back with his shoulders slightly open to the line of scrimmage, which will allow him to see his backside throughout his drop if he needs to. This will also allow him to easily throw to his backside without doing anything drastic at the end of his drop to compensate for poor drop mechanics. The quarterback is then able to see exactly what the defense is doing throughout his drop and is better able to anticipate when the receiver is going to break open.

Carrying the Ball High
with One or Both Elbows Sticking Out

This technique was probably taught when the quarterback was very young so he would have a quicker release (Figure 3-3). Again, this is bad for many reasons.

Figure 3-3.

- The ball is too far away from the body. A defender could easily knock it loose.

- The elbows are to high and away from the body. It would be hard to generate any speed or accuracy on the ball from this position.

First, the quarterback will tend to push the ball because of the position his hands are in. Try it yourself! You won't be able to put much velocity on the ball and you will have a tendency to drop your elbow when throwing the ball.

Second, it is hard to drop back or to run with the ball with your elbows sticking out. Running will cause the ball to shift back and forth because you are trying to balance yourself; there's a pendulum affect. It is hard to throw when the ball is moving all across your body.

Third, the defenders have an easy target to knock the ball loose. Keeping the ball high is like carrying a trophy around in your pocket; everyone can get a piece of it.

Finally, it will force the quarterback to have tense shoulders. This will have an adverse effect on his throwing mechanics.

The correct way for the quarterback to carry the ball is to have it chest high with the points of the ball vertical. He will have his elbows in and close to the body but not touching. The top end of the ball should be just about level with the top of his sternum. The ball should be carried smoothly, with very little motion away from the center of his body. The will obviously protect the ball and help the quarterback to drop back or move in the pocket more smoothly and efficiently. It is also easier and more efficient to throw the football from this position. Try it; you will notice the difference.

Quarterback Difficulty, Cause, & Correction Checklist

Difficulty	Probable Cause	Suggested Correction
You are dropping the snap during the exchange.	Your hands are coming apart during the exchange. This is very common. Also, you could be leaning back with your upper body as you receive the snap from center.	You must focus on keeping your hands in the proper position and keep them together during the exchange. The coach should watch your hands during the exchange to make sure this is happening.
You are slipping at the end of your drop.	You may be rushing your drops. Your strides are probably too long near the end of the drop.	You must shorten your stride towards the end of your drop into control-type steps. The first two-thirds of the drop should be long strides with the remaining one-third made up of shorter, control-type steps.
You are throwing the ball too short or into the ground.	You are probably overstriding. This causes you to lock out your front knee, which causes the front shoulder to drop down.	Shorten your target-step stride so you can keep your shoulders level during the throw. You must land heal to toe with a flexed knee as your throw the pass.
You are throwing the ball high over the target.	Your shoulders are pointed upward during the throw because your momentum has taken the weight of your upper body behind your plant foot.	You should drop your front shoulder at the end of the drop to stabilize and level your shoulders for the throw.
You are throwing behind the receivers on sideline routes – especially to your backside. Also, you are throwing behind the receivers on slants and crossing routes.	Your plant foot is not perpendicular to your target area. Your target step is not pointed to the area where the ball and the target will meet.	Concentrate on placing your plant-step in the proper position for the throw. In addition, your target foot needs to be pointed to where you want the ball to go–not where the target is as you throw the pass.
The receivers are always dropping your passes.	You have poor ball placement and you are probably throwing the ball too hard when the receivers are not that far from you.	Throwing the ball hard is not necessary at certain times. Anticipate when the receiver is breaking open and throw it before this occurs. Then throw a pass with great rotation that is easy to catch.

Quarterback Difficulty, Cause, & Correction Checklist

Difficulty	Probable Cause	Suggested Correction
• You are throwing passes that wobble.	• Your grip may need adjusting. It may be too tight.	• Experiment with different grips until you find one that corrects this problem. In addition, your grip may be too tight on the football.
• You deep balls are wobbly and don't turn over.	• Again your grip may be too tight, and you may be palming the ball. Also, your mechanics may be incorrect. Your shoulders may not be in the correct position. You may have held on to the ball too long before the throw.	• Loosen your grip on the football. Throw the ball on time so that you don't have to try and throw the ball too hard. Take a 5-quick with a hitch-step and let it go on time. Also, make sure your shoulders are pointed upwards so that the ball takes off at the proper instant. Don't overstride, and try to follow through.
• You are throwing bad passes on rollouts and on boot action.	• Your body is probably not in the best throwing position just before the throw. You may be tensing up your upper body as your throw the football.	• Make sure you are running towards where you want the football to go. Your hips need to be square to the target and you should step at the target as your throw the football. Also, breathe out and relax as you throw the pass.
• Your arm and shoulder are sore.	• First, you are probably gripping the football too tight when you throw. In addition, your mechanics may be currently inferior. If something is wrong with your mechanics, the rest of your body will try and compensate for it.	• Again, loosen your grip on the football. Also, you may need rest. You should always warm down after throwing and pack your arm in ice after a heavy day of throwing. Work on your mechanics in the off-season. Poor mechanics is probably the number-one cause of arm and shoulder problems with young quarterbacks.

Standing Too Tall in the Pocket

When you do this, especially while standing in one place going through your progressions, it makes passing difficult when your knees are locked out straight (Figure 3-4). In addition, you tend to tense up while you are attempting to get as tall as you can in the pocket, and this also causes poor throwing mechanics.

Figure 3-4. This is a common problem that quarterbacks have. This is not a good position to be in when you want to throw a good pass.

- The key here is that the quarterback's knees are locked out. He will have trouble controlling the direction of the pass. It will have a tendency to be thrown into the ground, short of the target.

A better way to handle yourself in the pocket is to maintain a *compact* posture with your knees flexed. This makes it easier to deliver the ball with accuracy and velocity, and also makes it much easier to move around the pocket if necessary.

Summary of Common Flaws in Quarterback Mechanics

- When the quarterback has poor hand placement while under center, it will lead to more fumbled snaps.
- When the quarterback drops back too fast, it will result in poor mechanics and an inability to throw to any backside target.
- When the quarterback carries the ball too high with his elbows out, it will lead to poor control and speed on passes.
- When the quarterback stands too tall in the pocket, it will lead to passes being thrown into the ground.

CHAPTER 4

Defensive Coverages and Fronts

Introduction

It is very beneficial for a quarterback to know what the various defensive coverages and fronts are designed to do. Every defensive coverage has own its strengths and weaknesses that can be exploited by the offense. Although defensive coordinators have devised a number of relatively exotic defenses in recent years, most defenses involve the following base coverages: cover 3 zone, cover 2 zone, or cover 2 man; quarters – a coverage that is has either a man concept or a bracket concept depending on the release of the number two receiver; and finally, man-to-man.

Coverages are designed to limit the productivity of certain offensive concepts. A well-rounded and diverse offense can take immediate advantage of the defense by knowing how to attack it in a sound and productive way. For example, cover 2 zone can hurt the productivity of an offense's quick-passing game. However, this defense can be vulnerable to routes that break open further downfield as long as the corners are anchored to their respective zones by putting a receiver in the flat area.

The quarterback who is cognizant of this fact can immediately audible the appropriate pass play that will take advantage of this concept and create a big play for his offense. The quarterback who knows the concepts of defense can watch a tape of an upcoming opponent and increase the probability of this kind of outcome.

Cover 3 Zone

Cover 3 zone is a fundamentally sound defense (Figure 4-1). However, as long as the offense is patient, it should be able to *nickel and dime* its way down the field. A lot of areas on the field can be attacked provided the receivers run disciplined routes and the quarterback knows where to go with the football. The second-level coverage (the linebackers) has only four defenders available to cover the field horizontally. This means that the areas on the field that an offense can take advantage of. Curl routes, dig routes, sideline routes, and double square-in patterns are all appropriate to call Vs in this type of coverage. Although it is unlikely that an offense can throw deep attacking from a standard offensive set, a four-receiver set with all four receivers running go routes with good spacing can create an immediate big play.

Figure 4-1. Cover 3 Zone.

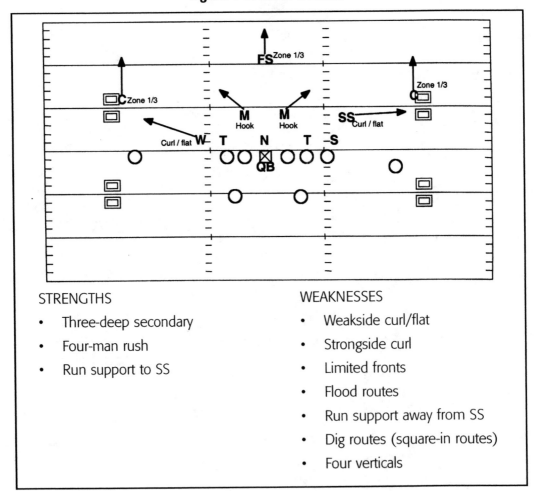

STRENGTHS

- Three-deep secondary
- Four-man rush
- Run support to SS

WEAKNESSES

- Weakside curl/flat
- Strongside curl
- Limited fronts
- Flood routes
- Run support away from SS
- Dig routes (square-in routes)
- Four verticals

Cover 2 Zone

Cover 2 zone is another basic defense that can disrupt the timing of the quick-passing game (Figure 4-2). This is because five defenders at the second level are no longer defending the field horizontally to a depth of approximately 12 yards from the line of scrimmage.

Additionally, the outside receivers can have the route disrupted because the cornerbacks are taught to jam the outside receiver as he passes by his zone. However, the deep coverage could then be compromised down the sideline and deep down the middle of the field by an astute offense.

By sending one receiver deep to the outside, another receiver deep down the middle, and a third receiver in the flat, the defense has only two defenders to cover the three different areas that the receivers currently occupy. This can be damaging to the defense in that these types of completions are usually big plays that gain substantial yards.

Figure 4-2. Cover 2 Zone.

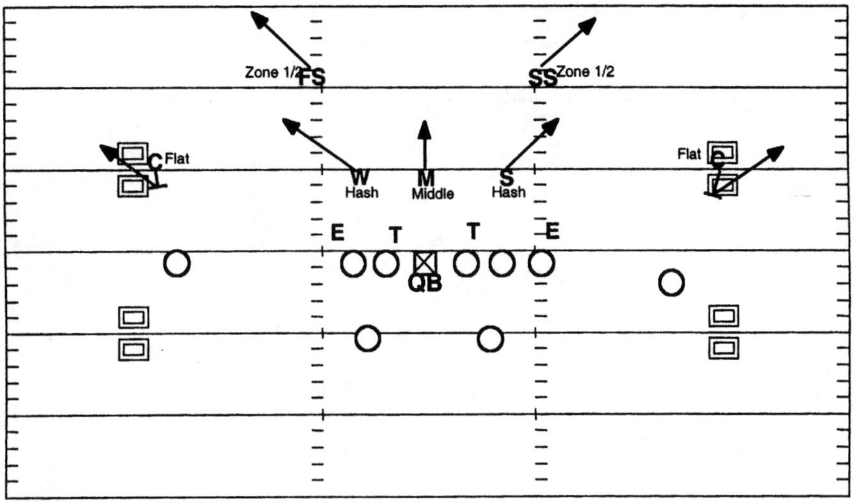

STRENGTHS

- Five underneath coverage
- Ability to disrupt timing of outside receivers with "jam"
- Can rush four
- Flat areas

WEAKNESSES

- Deep coverages
  √ fade area
  √ deep middle
- Strongside curl
- Run support off-tackle

Quarters Coverage

Quarters coverage is one of the more recent innovations in defenses today (Figure 4-3). Generally speaking, this type of defense has the ability to double cover an offense's outside receivers on medium to deep-pass routes. This type of coverage also allows the two safeties to become more of a factor on run support, but it is susceptible in the flat areas of the field. This is because the outside linebackers are responsible for covering that area of the field. In addition, you can nullify the safety help covering the outside receivers by running inside receivers at the safeties. This usually converts the coverage to a man-to-man type of defense as far as the defensive backfield is concerned. Furthermore, play-action fakes directed at one of the safeties can make this coverage vulnerable to a throw over the top of that safety.

Figure 4-3. Quarters Coverage.

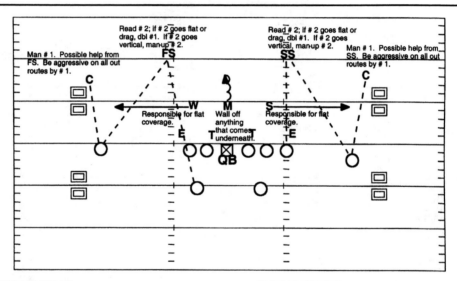

STRENGTHS

- Four-deep coverage
- Run support from safeties
- Ability to double cover outside receivers
- Allows corners to play aggressive technique on outside receivers because they have help over-the-top from safeties

WEAKNESSES

- Flat coverage
- Safeties are very susceptible to play-action
- Double coverage on #1 can be nullified by having #2 attack the coverage of safety

Cover 1 Free

Whenever a defense goes into any kind of man coverage, you can expect some type of blitz. Versus cover 1 free, crossing routes can be very productive provided you have the extra rusher(s) blocked (Figure 4-4). In addition, fade routes run by the outside receivers, or even four-vertical patterns run by the receivers, can be big plays as long as you throw away from the free safety.

Figure 4-4. Cover 1 Free.

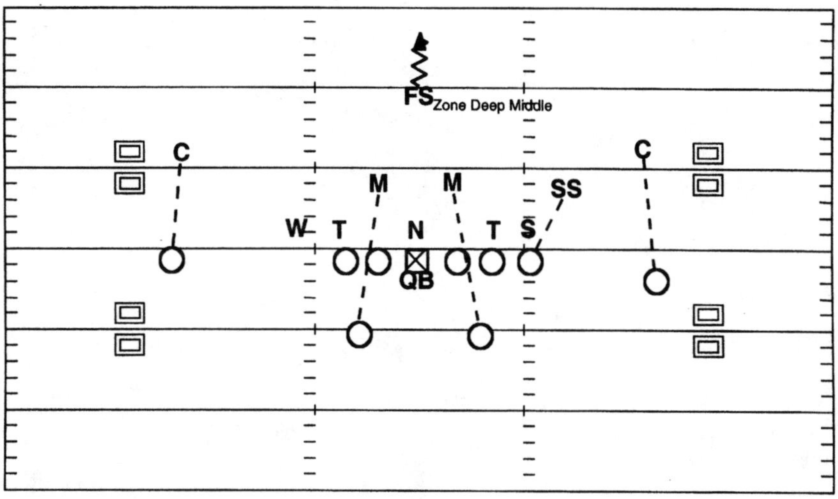

STRENGTHS	WEAKNESSES
• Help in the deep middle	• No underneath help
• Tight coverage	√ crossing routes
• Good run support to SS	√ breaking routes
• Can rush five	√ pick routes
	• Play-action passes
	• Out routes

Cover Zero Man

Versus cover zero man, expect more rushers than you can block with conventional pass protection. Some teams could even bring seven or even eight defenders at once. Although this is fundamentally unsound because they can't have all your possible receivers accounted for, it could cause a big play defensively if you think you have the time to drop back and wait for one of your receivers to break open downfield.

Figure 4-5. Cover Zero Man.

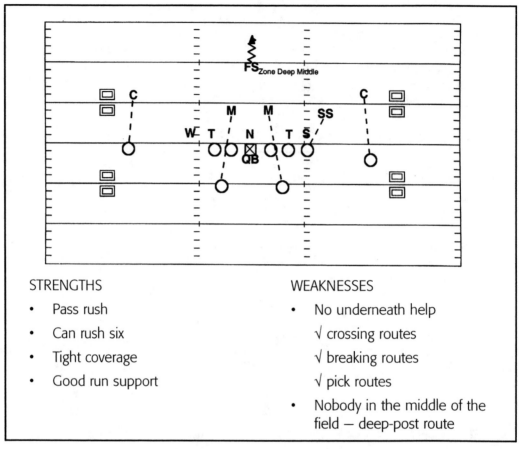

STRENGTHS

- Pass rush
- Can rush six
- Tight coverage
- Good run support

WEAKNESSES

- No underneath help
  √ crossing routes
  √ breaking routes
  √ pick routes
- Nobody in the middle of the field — deep-post route

You have to have a play ready before the ball is even snapped. You can audible to a quick *slide* protection to wash the extra defenders down, or change the protection to a maximum protection scheme. Some offenses have built-in hot routes that should break open immediately and be very effective against this defense. Again, crossing routes are effective as well as routes that are run vertically down the field as long as you can get the pass off before the rush gets to you.

Basic Defensive Fronts and Terminology

The following are the most basic terms used when describing defensive fronts. Although different names exist for these fronts, these are the most generic terms possible to give some insight into how offenses see and label defensives.

For example, although the weakside outside linebacker is called *Will* in this terminology, that same linebacker might be called *Whip* or perhaps *Wanda* in someone else's terminology. The important thing to remember is who the weakside linebacker is and what probable responsibilities he might have.

It is important to know that both the linemen and the linebackers usually have some type of *gap* responsibility. That means that the defenders *in the box* are responsible for specific areas between the offensive linemen (Figure 4-7). To cover those areas, the defenders have to line up within the same general area as their responsibilities dictate (Figure 4-8).

The dashed lined area is generally what is considered the box Figure (4-6). This is an area covering roughly just outside where the tight end would line up in width, and about four to six yards from the line of scrimmage in depth.

Figure 4-6. This is a graphic representation of the different *gaps* that are designated by letters.

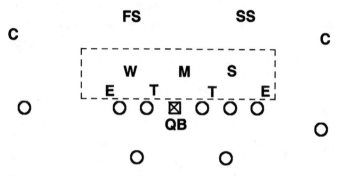

Figure 4-7. This is a graphic representation of the techniques (position relative to a specific lineman or area) that the defenders can line up in. For example, when it is said that the defender lined up in a *7 technique*, that means he lined up on the inside shade of the tight end.

D C B A A B C D

O O O ⊠ O O O

QB

Figure 4-8. This is important because a defender usually lines up relative to his area of responsibility. For example, if the defender lined up in a *3 technique*, he is most likely responsible for the *B gap*.

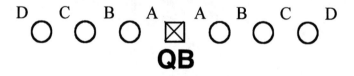

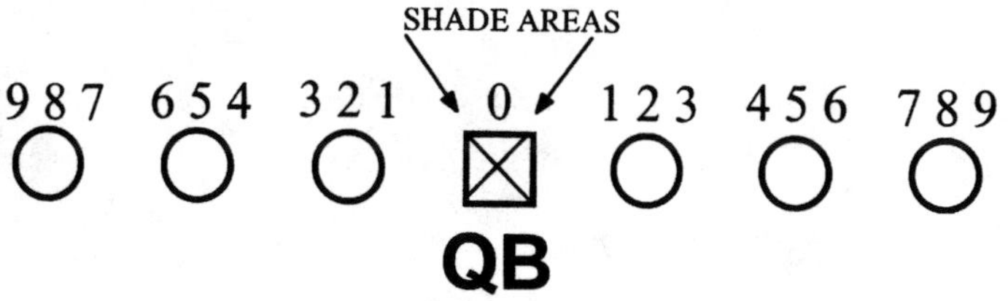

Odd Fronts

Odd Front: A down lineman is over the center (Figure 4-9).

Figure 4-9.

N
⊠
QB

Basic 50 Front: In this front, the three true down linemen (a noseguard and two tackles) and an outside linebacker (an end) on the strongside that will be in a three-point stance and rush most of the time. The outside linebacker on the weakside usually drops into coverage on pass plays but acts as an end on running plays. The two middle backers – *Meg* (weakside) and *Mike* (strongside) – are also present (Figure 4-10).

Figure 4-10.

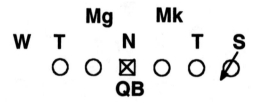

Bear Front: This is when both guards and the center are covered by down linemen and the strong safety is at this point in the box, giving us *eight* men in the box. The linebackers have to compensate some as well (Figure 4-11).

Figure 4-11.

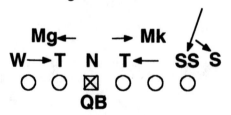

Eagle: This is when both guards and the center are covered by down linemen. This is sometimes called a *double eagle.* Please note that seven men are in the box (Figure 4-12).

Figure 4-12.

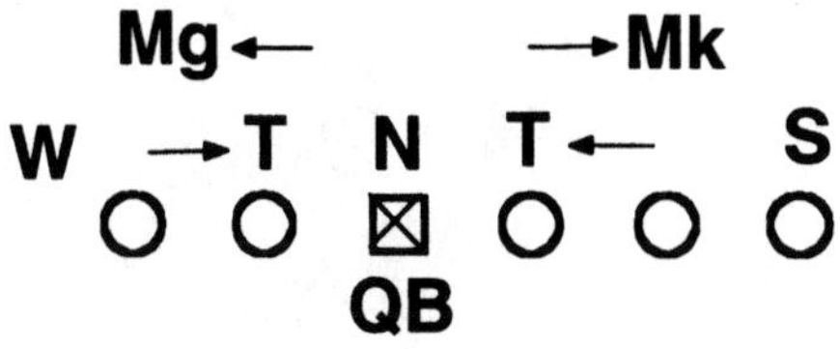

```
Mg←          →Mk
W  →T  N  T←    S
   O  O  ⊠  O  O  O
         QB
```

Eagle Weak: This is when the center and weakside guard are covered by down linemen. The weakside tackle and *Will* backer (end) shift down. Meg adjusts to compensate (Figure 4-13).

Figure 4-13.

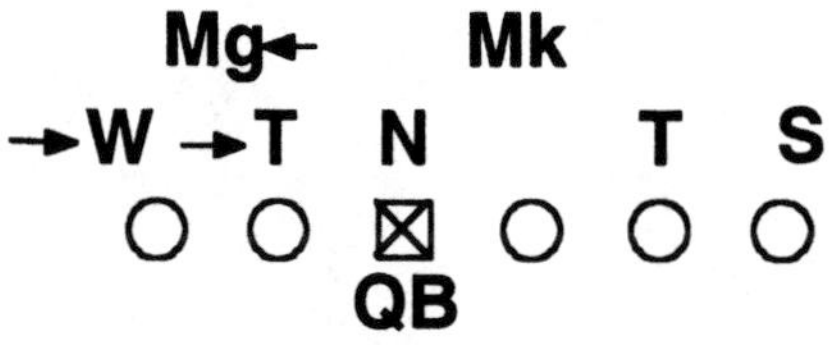

```
Mg←      Mk
→W →T  N       T  S
   O  O  ⊠  O  O  O
         QB
```

Eagle Strong: This is when the center and strongside guard are covered by down linemen. The strongside tackle will shift down over the guard, and the *Mike* linebacker will then compensate (Figure 4-14).

Figure 4-14.

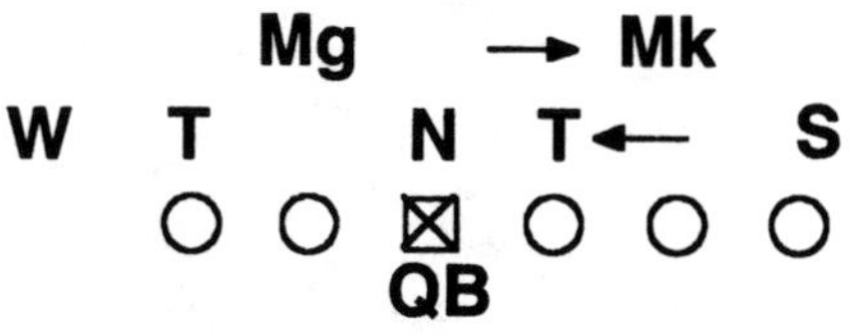

```
Mg    → Mk
W  T    N  T←  S
   O  O  ⊠  O  O  O
         QB
```

Reduced (see also Eagle Weak): The weakside tackle (in an odd front) slides down from covering the tackle and then covers the guard. The weakside outside linebacker will come down and cover the tackle. The Meg backer will adjust to compensate (Figure 4-15).

Figure 4-15.

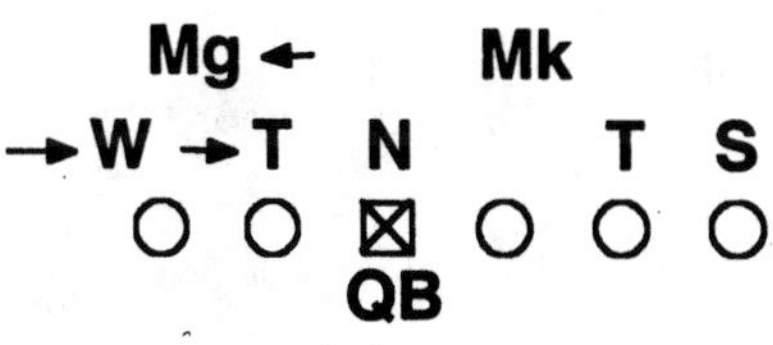

```
Mg ←      Mk
→W →T  N       T  S
   O  O  ⊠  O  O  O
         QB
```

Even Fronts

Even Front: No down lineman is covering the center (Figure 4-16).

Figure 4-16.

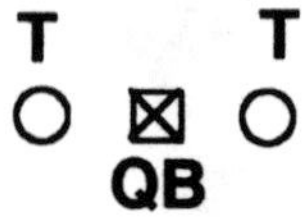

Basic 43 Front: This is when four down linemen (two tackles and two ends) and three linebackers: *Will* – the weakside outside linebacker, *Mike* – the inside linebacker, and *Sam* – the strongside outside linebacker – are all present (Figure 4-17).

Figure 4-17.

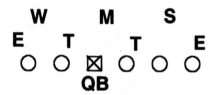

Over: This is when the weakside tackle (in an even front) shifts over the center and the weakside end shifts down. The Sam, Mike, and Will backers also shift to compensate (4-18).

Figure 4-18.

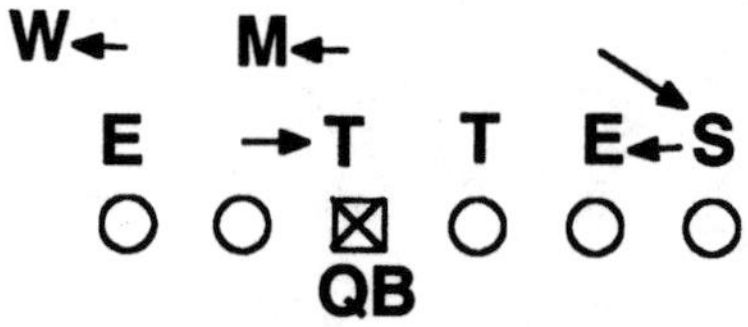

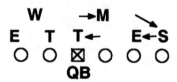

Under: This is when the strongside tackle and end (in an even front) shift to the weakside over the center and strongside tackle, and the Sam backer then comes up over the tight end and the Mike backer compensates (4-19).

Figure 4-19.

W   →M
E T T← E←S
○ ○ ⊠ ○ ○ ○
QB

CHAPTER 5

Quarterback Reads

Introduction

To be as productive as possible, the quarterback must learn a number of basic reads – both against zone coverage and man coverage. These basic reads allow the quarterback to throw just about any route combination in today's modern passing game. Mastering the material in this section should make it easier for the quarterback to come to the line of scrimmage, picture the pass pattern in his mind, and make the appropriate choice in receivers based on the defense – *in theory.*

The reality is much different. Quarterbacks need to know their own offense, they must study many hours of tape, and they must get a great deal of repetitions in practice and in games to be able to read a defense correctly, and then throw to the appropriate receiver *when the bullets are flying.*

Usually when quarterbacks first start trying to read defenses, everything happens so quickly, the quarterback is just trying to get the pass off to someone who might be open. Then, after hundreds of repetitions, both mentally and especially physically things start to slow down in the quarterback's mind. He begins to be able to see things happen in what some have termed *slow motion.* It doesn't happen overnight and it takes a great deal of work beyond the practice field. One day the *light will go on* and the quarterback will *get it.*

Several teaching methods can help accelerate this process. Of course, the quarterback should know his offense and what the offense is trying to do schematically. Drawing defenses on the board and knowing what the individual defender's responsibilities are, and then watching that defense on film, are also extremely helpful.

Once he does take the field, the use of 7-on-7 pass skeleton drills are very helpful in seeing what is going on downfield. Also, 4-on-4 pass skeleton drills (involving the only the backs and tight end going against the linebackers) are beneficial. 1-on-1 drills are good for teaching ball placement, as long as the quarterback doesn't stand in the pocket waiting for the receiver to finally break open.

Finally, young quarterbacks learn reading defenses by breaking the process down to smaller components. Teach them to read areas of the field first – and only two receivers at a time. For example, you should include a pattern that will have one receiver breaking across the middle at a depth of 16 yards, while another receiver runs a drag route across the middle of the field at four yards (a *drag-dig read*). The quarterback basically just reads the drop of the inside linebackers and has a one to two progression. Once he has mastered this, you should incorporate a receiver running a deep (or *alert*) route into the same the play. The quarterback will then take a peak at the receiver running the deep route before he shifts his eyes to the drag-dig read. This turns into a *one* to *two* to *three* progression for the quarterback. Then you should put a back delaying to a position over the middle at four yards so the quarterback has a *dump-off* at the end of his progression, if it is appropriate.

Of course, not that many pass patterns exist that will have a *one, two, three, dump-off* progression, and many pass patterns will only be a simple one, two progression; but this teaching sequence helps to keep the quarterbacks comfortable within the passing system.

Summary of Introduction

- In order for a quarterback to be productive, he must know how to read defenses.
- A quarterback must know his offense.
- A quarterback must study tapes and get lots of reps in practice.
- Although everything happens so fast when quarterbacks begin learning to read defenses, there comes a point when things start to happen in *slow motion*.
- A combination of drills helps the quarterback learn to read defenses.
- You should start the teaching progression with an area of the field to read and only a two progression read for the quarterback.
- Then you should move on by incorporating a deep or *alert* route into the pattern and the read, as well as a *dump-off* if appropriate.

Leverage Reads

The first thing you should do is teach the quarterback to what to read based on the defensive leverage – the defender's physical position relative to the receiver, and the route the receiver is going to run. For example, if a receiver is going to run a sideline route, and the defender is covering the receiver off and to the inside of the receiver, you would say that the defender has poor leverage relative to the route the receiver is going to run. You would want to throw to this receiver in this situation.

However, if that same receiver was going to run a post pattern, and the defender was in the same position of being off the receiver and to the inside -- right in the path that your receiver is going to run -- you would say that the defender has great leverage on your receiver relative to the route your receiver is going to run. In this case, you would not want to throw to this receiver at that time.

By reading the pre-snap alignment of the defense, the quarterback can get a pretty good idea of which two or three receivers he has a chance to complete the pass to. Only at the highest level of play can a defense really move quickly enough to disguise where they have to be in coverage.

To teach the leverage concept to the quarterback, you should have them learn and throw the quick-passing game first in the teaching progression. You should do this because the quarterback normally has to look at both sides and then decide which side, based on the defensive leverage, is the best side to attack. Then it is a matter of taking a three-step drop and deciding which of two receivers to throw to based on the movement of the defense, or the individual matchup.

When you teach the basic reads to a quarterback, you should teach the reads that concern the underneath coverage first, because most young quarterbacks have been focused on what happens with the third-level defenders (the secondary). The following are several pre-snap leverage examples (Figures 5-1 through 5-9).

Summary of Leverage Reads

- The quarterback must learn the defender's physical position relative to the receiver or the area the receiver is going to run to.
- The quick-passing game really helps the quarterback learn how to judge leverage.
- Teaching the quarterback *underneath* coverage reads should be first.

Leverage Read of the Quick Hitch

The receiver to the right would be the correct throw due to the defender's leverage and depth. He would have to go through the receiver to make the play. The left corner has the inside leverage and is in a better position to make the play.

Figure 5-1. Leverage read of the quick hitch.

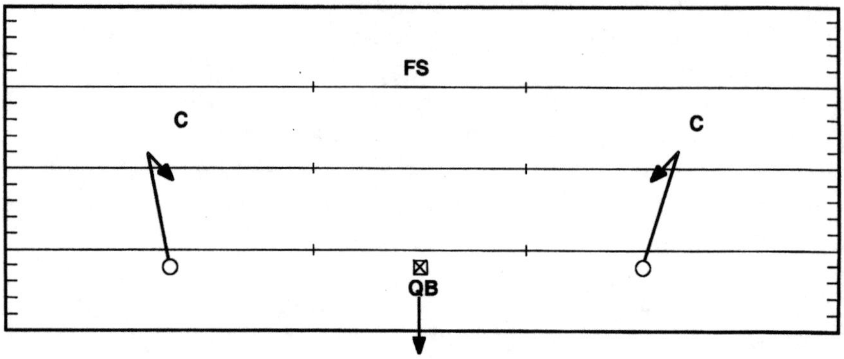

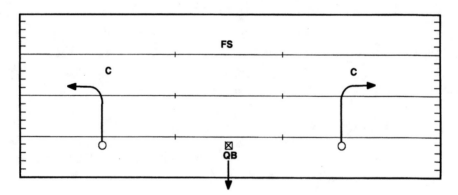

Leverage Read of the Quick Out

The receiver to the left would be the correct throw due to the defenders leverage and depth. The left corner has the inside leverage and would have a difficult time making the play.

Figure 5-2. Leverage read of the quick out.

Leverage Read of the Quick Slant

The receiver to the left would be the correct throw. Although the corners have equal leverage, the strong safety has a better angle to get into the passing lane. There is a much better throwing lane on the left. See Figure 5-3.

Figure 5-3. Leverage read of the quick slant.

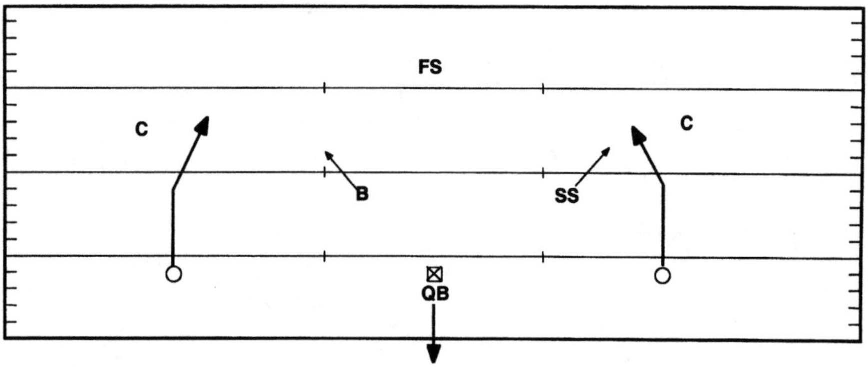

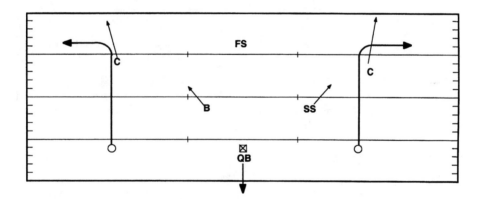

Leverage Read of the 12-Yard Speed Out

The receiver to the left would be the correct throw. The corner on the left has an inside-out leverage. He is giving up the out. The backer on the left side can't get into the passing lane.

Figure 5-4. Leverage read of the 12-yard speed out.

Leverage Read of the 12-Yard Curl

The receiver to the right would be the appropriate throw. The corner on the left has the inside-out leverage and therefore has the leverage on the route. The corner on the right side has the outside leverage and the strong safety and would most likely be pulled out of the passing lane by a flat or swing route to that side. See Figure 5-5.

Figure 5-5. Leverage read of the 12-yard curl.

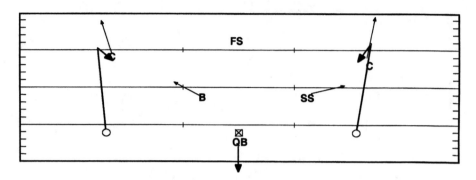

Leverage Read of the 18-Yard Comeback

The receiver to the left would be the appropriate throw. The corner on the left is playing deeper and is making sure he will not get beat deep. The corner on the right is playing a little tighter.

Figure 5-6. Leverage read of the 18-yard comeback.

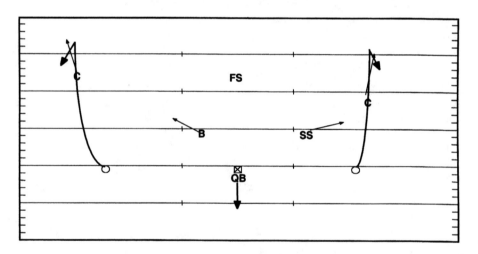

Leverage Read of the Post-Corner

The receiver to the right would be the appropriate throw. The right corner is playing the receiver tighter than the corner on the left and is more susceptible to a counter route. The corner on the left is playing deep outside and most likely will not bite on the post move. See Figure 5-7.

Figure 5-7. Leverage read of the post-corner.

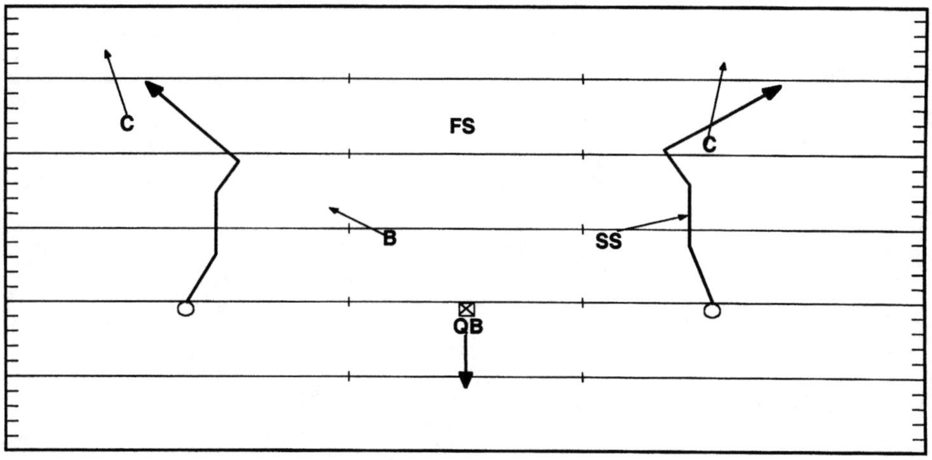

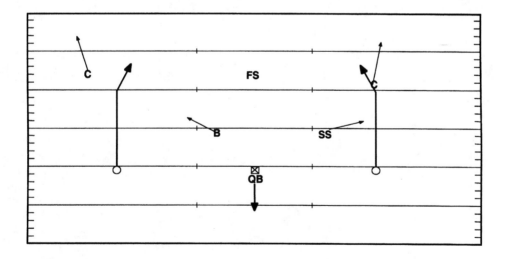

Leverage Read of the 12-Yard Skinny Post

The receiver to the left would be the appropriate throw. The left corner is playing deep outside and is giving up the skinny post. The underneath coverage is not in a position to get into the throwing lane. The free safety should be looked off before the throw.

Figure 5-8. Leverage read of the 12-yard skinny post.

Leverage Read of the Take-off or Streak

The receiver to the right would be the appropriate throw. The right corner is playing more heads up and tighter than the left corner. The left corner is playing deep outside and protecting his deep third. See Figure 5-9.

Figure 5-9. Leverage read of the take-off or streak.

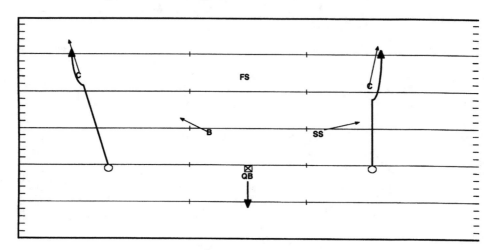

Reading Coverage and Going Through Progressions

Once the quarterback is aware of the fundamentals of leverage, you should break down the different coverage reads. The basic reads can then be incorporated into almost any number of more complex reads. As an example, a typical pattern breakdown will look something like the play in Figure 5-10.

Figure 5-10.

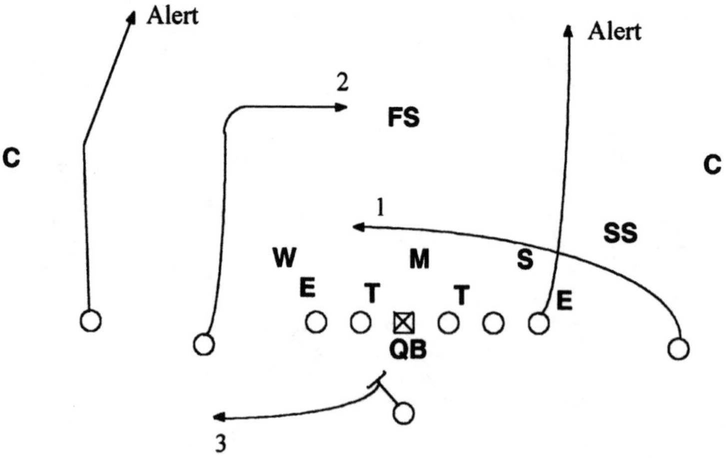

This can be a fairly complex play for a new quarterback. He has to decide if he has a chance to throw to the post or the up route vs. the defense (deep read). He must then decide if he has a chance to throw to either the dig route or the drag route (dig read) before looking to the back running a swing route out of the backfield (Figure 5-11).

Figure 5-11.

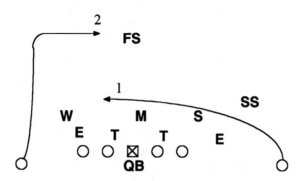

First you should isolate and teach the dig read within the pattern. You shouldn't focus on the vertical components of the pattern at this time. The quarterback must understand what the pattern is designed to do and what the progression is. Basically, the progression of a pattern is based on which receiver should be open first. Then, if that first receiver is not open, which receiver should be open second, and then which receiver should be open next – many times this third receiver will be called an *outlet* or a *dump-off*.

In many offenses, the first receiver to open up first is really running his route to bait the defense to jump that receiver, thereby leaving the number two receiver in the progression wide open. This pattern is illustrated in the previous figure. The receiver running the drag route is the first progression for the quarterback. If the linebackers come up to cover this drag route, they are not dropping to their area deeper downfield at approximately 12 yards. The dig route should make his break over the middle slightly later. Since the linebackers have come up to cover the drag route, the dig route will then be open. In other words, the quarterback will read the second level (linebackers). If they drop, he will give the ball to the drag route. If they jump the drag route, he will go to the dig route. Once he has mastered this read, you can incorporate the deep read into the progression (Figure 5-12).

Figure 5-12.

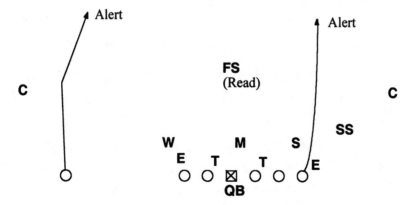

At this point, you can assume the quarterback knows where all the routes are going to be in this pattern. When he comes to the line of scrimmage and sees cover 3, he should know that he may have a chance at either the skinny-post route or the up route (deep read). He will make his decision by the third step in his drop. If the leverage is right, he will give the ball to either the post or the up route based on which way the free safety moves – he should throw away from the free safety. If for some reason during his drop, the quarterback doesn't like his chances with either of the vertical routes (deep read), he will focus his attention on the dig read within the pattern, and then, if time permits, his back running the swing route to the left.

However, if during the pre-snap read, the quarterback sees four-across, he will forget about the vertical (deep read) routes and go immediately to the dig read, and then to his running back (Figure 5-13).

Figure 5-13.

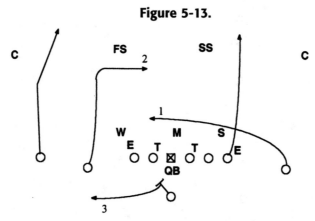

The quarterback will eventually learn which of the five possible receivers should get the ball in any given pass play based on a pre-snap read and what is going on during his five-step drop. However, you should be teaching the quarterback basic two-receiver reads at the beginning of the teaching progression, and then moving on to incorporate multiple reads within the pass pattern as he becomes comfortable within the system. This *teaching progression* assures that the quarterback has every opportunity to be successful within the offense.

Summary of Reading Coverage and Going Through Progression

- You should take any given pass pattern that may or may not be fairly complex.
- You should isolate the pattern into smaller components or basic reads.
- You should teach the quarterback the design and progression of the pattern.
- You should build or augment the reads once the quarterback has mastered the basic read within the pass pattern.
- The teaching progression will assure that the quarterback has every opportunity to be successful within the offense.

Basic Zone Reads

When the quarterback breaks the huddle, he has a standard procedure he must follow before and during each pass play — the pre-snap read and what he must do during his dropback.

Quarterback Pre-Snap

- You should always get to the line quickly with your hands under the center.
  - √ If the defense is going to shift, they will do it after you get under the center.
- You should look for the safeties.
  - √ Is there anyone in the middle of the field?
- You should look for the best side to read.
  - √ Based on the number of defenders vs. the number of receivers
  - √ Based on the defender's leverage
    - ♦ Leverage refers to the defender's relationship to the receiver, or the area of the field the defender must cover relative to where the routes are going to be run.
- You get a picture in your mind of where all the routes are going to be run.
- You should identify possible blitzes.
  - √ You should know where your hot routes are.

During The Dropback

- You should realize you are making the decision on where to go with the ball on your way back — not at the end of your drop.
  - √ If you haven't made a decision by the time you get to the end of your drop, go to the contingency plan right away.
    - ♦ With the exception of a quick three-step drop, take two shuffle-steps up in the pocket (maximum), before going to the contingency plan.
      - – For example, you've made a decision on where to go with the ball and you're waiting for the receiver to break away from the defender.

Quick-Slant Read

- The quarterback should key the flat defender.
  - √ Outside linebacker, strong safety, or cornerback

- The quarterback should throw away from the flat defender.
  - √ If the flat defender covers the slant, the quarterback should hit the flat/swing route.
  - √ If he goes flat, the quarterback should hit the slant.

Figure 5-14. The quick-slant read.

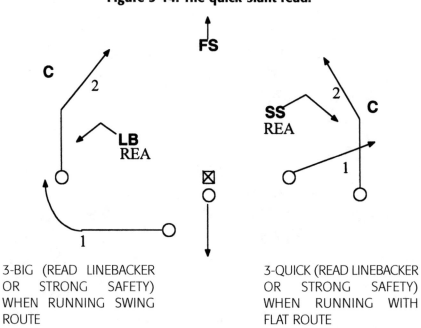

3-BIG (READ LINEBACKER OR STRONG SAFETY) WHEN RUNNING SWING ROUTE

3-QUICK (READ LINEBACKER OR STRONG SAFETY) WHEN RUNNING WITH FLAT ROUTE

The Quick-Slant Pass Drop

The quick-slant read should be the first read you teach. The drop will be slightly different depending on what the number two receiver is doing. When the number two receiver is running a swing route, the linebacker covering the flat usually takes more of a horizontal path to the flat area so the quarterback will go a little deeper in his drop to let the backer clear the passing lane.

When the number two receiver runs a flat route, the linebacker usually takes a more aggressive angle to cover the flat area. The quarterback's drop should be a bit quicker so he can give the ball to the number two receiver right away if the backers leverage is poor.

This same read concept is also used on other reads such as on *curl reads* and *skinny-post reads*, so it is a good starting point in the teaching progression. The quarterback has to get a leverage read, plus make a decision by the time he hits his third step. This is an excellent teaching tool.

- The quarterback's specific drop is dependant on the flat defender's leverage.
  - √ If the flat defender is close to the line of scrimmage (Pro 4-3), the drop will be deeper (3-big) so the quarterback can throw behind him.
  - √ If the flat defender is way off the line of scrimmage (College 4-3), the drop will be shallower (3-quick) so the quarterback can throw in front of him.

The Stick Read

The *stick read* is a read that is not in all offenses, although it is a very high percentage throw that usually nets a minimum of five or more yards every time it's used. It is usually thrown with a wing back approximately one-yard outside the tight end and one-yard off the line of scrimmage running a flat route to draw the coverage away from the stick route.

However, it can also be utilized by having the running back starting in the backfield running a *shoot* route. The tight end will still run the stick route, and the running back will then run directly to where the wide receiver lined up looking over his inside shoulder.

The quarterback will look to the flat or shoot route first. If the strong safety has poor leverage or doesn't cover the flat area, the quarterback should give the ball to him right away and let him run after the catch. If the strong safety takes off to chase the flat or shoot route, he should give the ball to the tight end right away. This is an easy read to learn and gives the quarterback confidence because it is a rhythm throw.

Figure 5-15. The Stick Read   **Figure 5-16. The Stick Read**

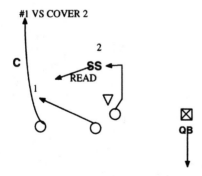

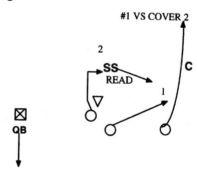

3-BIG HOLD (READ SS) TO GET STICK ROUTE OPEN, LOOK AT FLAT ROUTE FIRST.

3-BIG HOLD (READ SS) TO GET STICK ROUTE OPEN, LOOK AT FLAT ROUTE FIRST.

Summary of the Stick Read

- The quarterback should key the strong safety or the defender who will cover that area.
- The quarterback should check the pre-snap leverage.
- The quarterback should look for the flat, and then the stick.
  - √   Many times looking at the flat route first will open up the stick route.
- Versus cover 2, the quarterback should look to the strongside fade first.

The Inside-Sideline Read

The *inside-sideline* read is very similar to the stick read – the difference is that the quarterback will take a deeper drop. This is another way to get the tight end involved in the passing game as both the stick and the sideline routes are easy to complete.

This is a nice change up and gets the quarterback to read the patterns that develop over the tackle box. You should teach both the stick and inside-sideline reads with the use of a 4-on-4 drill. You should take the quarterback, both backs, and the tight end, and run a pass skeleton against the second-level defenders (the linebackers). This is an excellent way to teach the quarterback how to see and read the defense to consistently complete passes around the linebackers.

Figure 5-17. The inside-sideline read.   **Figure 5-18. The inside-sideline read.**

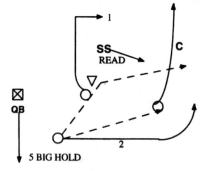

5 BIG HOLD (READ SS) TO GET TE ROUTE OPEN, LOOK AT SWING ROUTE FIRST.

5-BIG HOLD (READ SS) TO GET TE ROUTE OPEN, LOOK AT SWING ROUTE FIRST.

Summary of the Inside-Sideline Read

- The quarterback should key the strong safety or the defender who will cover that area.
- The quarterback should check the pre-snap leverage.
- The quarterback should look for the swing, and then the sideline.
  - √ Many times looking at the swing route first will open up the sideline route.

The Curl Read

The *curl read* is very similar to the quick-slant read in that the quarterback is still reading the flat defender. He is taking a deeper, 5-big with a hitch-step drop, and this helps him to see the play develop as the defenders drop to their respective zones.

Again, just like the quick-slant read, when the number two receiver is running a swing route, the linebacker covering the flat usually takes more of a horizontal path to the flat area. The quarterback should go a little deeper in his drop to let the backer clear the passing lane.

When the number two receiver runs a flat route, the linebacker usually takes a more aggressive angle to cover the flat area. Unlike the quick-slant read, the quarterback's drop will remain the same: a 5-big with a hitch drop.

Figure 5-19. The curl read.

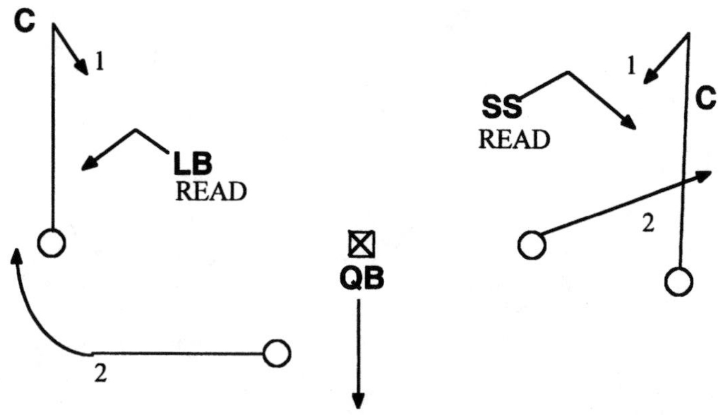

5-BIG HITCH (READ LINEBACKER OR STRONG SAFETY) TO GET CURL OPEN LOOK TO SWING OR FLAT FIRST.

Summary of the Curl Read

- The quarterback should key the flat defender.
  - √ Outside linebacker, strong safety, or cornerback
- The quarterback should throw away from the flat defender.
  - √ If the defender goes flat, the quarterback should hit the curl.
  - √ If he drops to curl, the quarterback should hit the flat/swing route.

The Sideline Read

The *sideline read* is primarily used when the cornerbacks are playing off of the wide receiver. This is strictly a timing route and needs a good deal of practice repetitions for it to be effective. A pre-snap read of the leverage is critical.

As long as the cornerback is playing off of the receiver, the only defender able to stop the pass is the flat defender (usually the strong safety or outside linebacker). However, by running a receiver on some type of seam route, this defender can usually be taken out of the equation. Another component of the route is that it must be converted if the corner becomes the flat defender. This is sometimes called a *kick* defender or *squat* defender. It is imperative that the wide receiver take an outside release when this happens, and covert the sideline route into a fade route.

Figure 5-20. The sideline read.

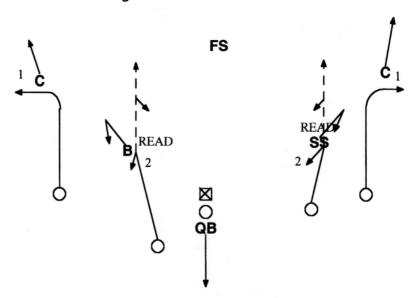

5-ROLL (READ LINEBACKER OR STRONG SAFETY)

Although this *built-in* conversion makes the pattern sound, it is not advisable to call the sideline route versus situations where the defense would *kick* the coverage. Several better patterns are available to run versus this scenario. Sometimes the defense will only roll or kick the coverage into the short side of the field. When this happens, the quarterback should throw to the side of the field where the cornerback is playing off the receiver.

Summary of the Sideline Read

- Versus cover 2, the sideline will automatically turn into a fade route.
- The quarterback should check the corner and safety alignment.
- The quarterback should check the outside linebacker/strong safety alignment.
- The quarterback should key the flat defender.
  - √ Outside linebacker, strong safety, or cornerback
    - ♦ If the flat defender can get underneath the route or into the passing lane, the quarterback should throw to the stop or seam route.

The Deep-Out Read

The *deep-out read* can be used in a number of ways. Probably the best use of it is against cover 2 when you have two deep defenders and five underneath defenders. By sending a receiver to the flat area to hold the cornerback, you can then exploit the deep-out area by running an inside-release sideline route at 18-plus yards, or by running a corner route into the same general area.

Figure 5-21. The deep-out read.

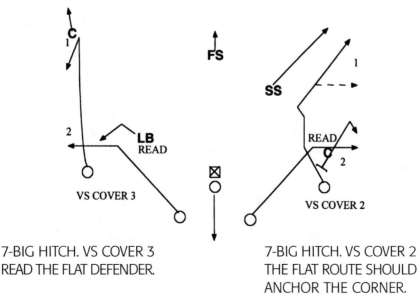

7-BIG HITCH. VS COVER 3
READ THE FLAT DEFENDER.

7-BIG HITCH. VS COVER 2
THE FLAT ROUTE SHOULD
ANCHOR THE CORNER.

Figure 5-22. The deep-out read.

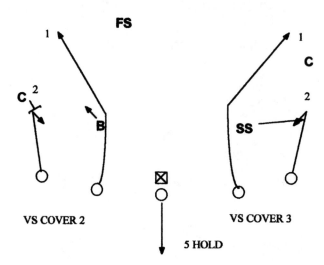

In addition, an offense can take advantage of the deep middle by sending the wide receivers vertical down the sideline, and an inside receiver down the middle of the field. As long as one cornerback is occupied in the flat area, the deep defenders are out numbered three to two.

Summary of the Deep-Out Read

- It is a great route versus cover 2.
  - √ The flat route will hold the corner.
    - ♦ If the corner runs with the wide receiver, the quarterback should hit the flat route right away.
    - ♦ If the corner comes off the wide receiver, the quarterback should continue his drop and hit the wide receiver on the deep out.

The Dig Read

The *dig read* can be a much easier read for a quarterback if he understands what the defensive responsibilities are, as well as what a particular defense does, to defend it the middle of the field.

The dig-read pass pattern has one receiver crossing the middle of the field at 15-plus yards, and another receiver crossing the field at less that five- yards depth. The second-level defenders (the linebackers) are put into a difficult position; if they drop to their zones at approximately 12-yards deep, the drag route will open up in front of them. If the linebackers come up to defend the drag route, the dig route will be open behind them.

To enhance the success of this route, a deep-post route should be included down the middle of the field to take the third-level defenders out of the play. Also, it is advisable that the defense be stretched horizontally as well by putting receivers into the flat areas by swinging them or sending them on flat routes.

Figure 5-23. The dig read.

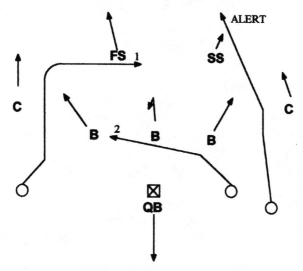

7-QUICK HITCH (READ INSIDE BACKER). TO GET DIG ROUTE OPEN, LOOK AT TIGHT END DRAG ROUTE FIRST.

Figure 5-24. The dig read.

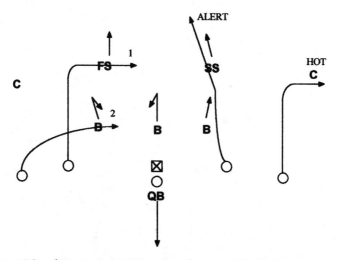

7-QUICK HITCH (READ INSIDE BACKER). TO GET DIG ROUTE OPEN, LOOK AT TIGHT END DRAG ROUTE FIRST.

Summary of the Dig Read

- The quarterback should key the underneath coverage.
  - √ While dropping back, the quarterback should take a look at what the linebackers are doing.
  - √ If they drop, the quarterback should hit the drag.
  - √ If they jump or wall the drag, the quarterback should go for the dig.

The Double Square-In Read

The *double square-in read* is different than the dig read in that the route will normally open up to the outside of the tackle box. The quarterback will take a pre-snap read at the free safety to see if any possibility exists that the post could be open. He will then drop back and key the second-level defenders.

If the strong safety moves horizontally to cover the back running to the flat, and the outside linebacker jumps or walls the tight end running the square-in route, the open receiver will be the wide receiver. The cornerback should not be a big factor in the play.

If either the strong safety or the outside linebacker drops to take away wide receiver's route, the quarterback should throw to the receiver they just left. This is a good play if you need to gain more than 10 yards verses a zone defense, and the read is similar to a combination of the dig and curl reads.

Figure 5-25. The double square-in read.

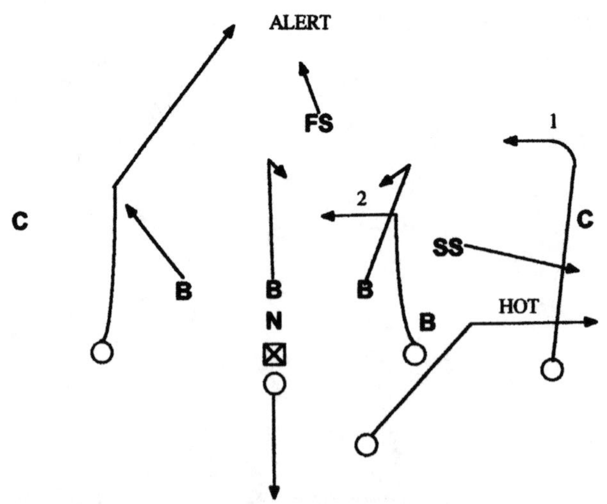

5-BIG HITCH (READ BACKER TO STRONG SAFETY). TO GET WIDE RECEIVER OPEN LOOK TO TIGHT END FIRST, RUNNING BACK LAST.

Figure 5-26. The double square-in read.

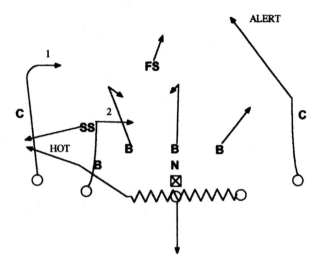

5-BIG HITCH (READ BACKER TO STRONG SAFETY). TO GET WIDE
RECEIVER OPEN LOOK TO TIGHT END FIRST, RUNNING BACK LAST.

Summary of the Double Square-In Read

- The quarterback should key the outside linebacker to the strong safety.
    - √ If the linebacker takes the medium square-in route and the strong safety takes the flat area, the quarterback should hit the deep square-in.
    - √ If either the linebacker or the strong safety takes away the deep square-in, the quarterback should throw to the area they vacate.

The Deep Read

This is a very popular pass read at most levels of football. However, it is also a very low percentage pass most of the time – unless the receivers are superior to the defensive backs, or the pass is set up well by the play caller.

If a quarterback *nickel and dimes* a defense, they generally have a tendency to come up to make the play. The defense anticipates and reacts. If an offense completes enough short passes in this fashion, the defense will usually become a bit frustrated and try to make a play on a receiver. They will play closer to the line of scrimmage to make the play. This is an excellent time to go deep on a defense. By being patient and by throwing the high-percentage passes most of the game, the offense has created more separation between the defense and the deep receivers, which increases the probability of completing the deep pass for a big gain, and quite possibly, a touchdown. The basic philosophy here is to take what the defense gives you. If they play off, throw underneath them until they come up and can't defend the deep pass.

Figure 5-27. The deep read.

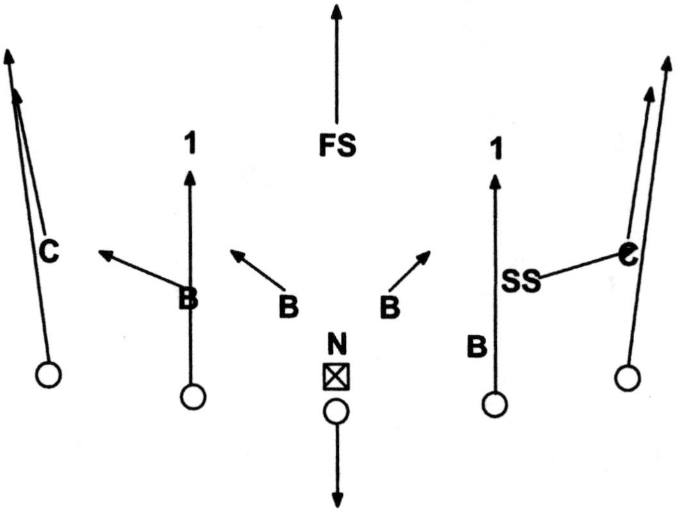

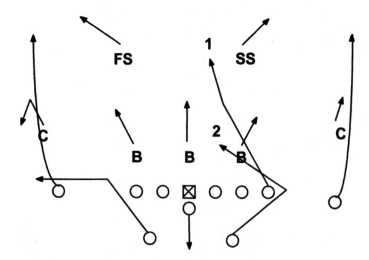

5-BIG HITCH (READ FREE). TO GET SLOT OPEN LOOK TO WIDE RECEIVER FIRST. HIT SLOT AS HE PASSES THE BACKER DROP.

Figure 5-28. The deep read.

5-BIG HITCH (READ FREE). LOOK TO THE SIDE THE BACK RELEASES TO (THIS WILL ANCHOR THE CORNER). TO GET TIGHT END OPEN LOOK TO WIDE RECEIVER FIRST. HIT TIGHT END AS HE PASSES THE BACKER DROP.

A pre-snap read is critical. Young quarterbacks have to have a fairly good idea of which side of the field they are going to throw to. Once that is decided, it is important that the quarterback throw the ball on time. Too often quarterbacks wait for the receiver to get open rather than anticipating which receiver will be open. When they hold to ball too long, the will underthrow the receiver and usually throw a wobbly pass because they are gripping the ball too tightly to throw the ball past their range.

A general rule would be to always throw the ball on time, and make the decision on where to go with the ball by the third step in the drop. If no clear decision appears on where to go with the ball, the quarterback should throw to an underneath outlet receiver, or pull the ball down and run for as many yards as he can get. However, being patient with the offense will increase the probability that the quarterback will complete the deep passes.

Summary of the Deep Read

- This is a timing pass.
- The quarterback should realize that deep passes are not high percentage completions.
- The quarterback should get a good idea where he has the best chance to go with the ball on his pre-snap read.
- If the quarterback is not sure where to go deep with the ball on his third step (of a five-step drop), he should let the ball go to an underneath receiver.
- Four verticals vs. cover 3
    - √ The inside seams are the quarterback's first read.
    - √ The quarterback should hit the seam route as he passes the linebackers at about 15 yards.
- The quarterback should look the safety off with a good look at the wide receivers as he drops.
    - √ The quarterback should throw away from the safety coverage.

CHAPTER 6

Shotgun Passing

Introduction

Running the offense from a shotgun formation generally makes the quarterback's job easier, even though it limits the offense in terms of what kind of running plays it can run. When the quarterback is standing five yards from the line of scrimmage, he can have a better vantage point to see the defense. He also has a *head start* as far as his drop is concerned, since he is already five yards from the line of scrimmage. Quarterbacks also have a better vantage point to see what is happening as far as their backside is concerned.

Unfortunately, the offense is somewhat limited in what types of plays can be run because the quarterback is detached from the center. The defense also takes a different posture when the quarterback is in the *gun*. Some quarterbacks who are used to running a timing-offense don't necessarily like playing in the gun because they don't have the same timing they do while dropping back from center. Although several colleges use the gun a great deal of the time, the NFL has yet to adopt such an offense that is run predominantly from the shotgun formation.

You can still have an aspect of precision when playing quarterback from the shotgun formation. Although the drops are different, the quarterback can still use good technique and play-action fakes, and will always have his shoulders level for the throw (the exception being the deep passes when the quarterback will pitch his shoulders slightly upward when throwing the football).

The Stance

The quarterback's stance in the shotgun formation is very different from when he lines up under the center. His feet will be staggered and he will have his right foot back (in a right-handed quarterback) with that same heel five yards from the line of scrimmage. The left foot will be placed slightly more than heel to toe in front of the back foot (Figure 6-1). This is done for several reasons.

First, the right foot is usually the dominant one in right-handed quarterbacks. To prove this, ask your quarterback how he would stand on a surfboard (or even a skate board). More often than not, he will place his left foot in front of his right. You want this dominant foot back in case of a bad snap. If the ball is low, it's much more natural for the quarterback to squat down and retrieve the ball with his left foot forward. If the ball is snapped off to the left, the quarterback will have an easier time opening up to the left side, and will cover more ground because his right foot is back. If the ball goes off to the right side, the quarterback is in a good position to almost run after the ball to catch it, since his hips are slightly open to the right side. Finally, if the ball is snapped high, the quarterback can jump off the dominant foot (the right foot).

In addition, when the quarterback takes his two- to four-step drop when receiving the ball from the gun, a smooth transition should occur going into the drop; he can easily bring his left foot back across his right foot in his first crossover step. This allows the quarterback to catch the snap first, and then glide into his drop in a smooth and efficient manner.

Figure 6-1. This is an example of a quarterback in the shotgun stance.

- The quarterback's arms are extended with a slight bend at the elbow to receive the snap from center.

- He has a slight bend at his waist.

- His knees are slightly flexed.

- His right heel is five yards from the line of scrimmage.

- His feet are staggered slightly more than heel to toe.

When the quarterback is in the gun and throwing a quick pass, he is also in the optimal position to catch the ball, find the open receiver, and then throw the pass with the proper mechanics in a smooth and efficient manner. It's important to remember that the quarterback will not have time to find the laces when throwing the quick passing game from the shotgun formation. He needs to catch the ball, grip it, and then let it go very quickly.

The Shotgun Quick-Passing Game

The quarterback will be throwing the quick-passing game from just over five-yards behind the line of scrimmage. You don't want the timing or mechanics of his throw to be altered very much.

For the five possible receivers, no difference exists in how they run their respective pass routes when throwing from the shotgun formation. The only differences for the quarterback are:

- He lines up five yards from the line of scrimmage instead of under the center.
- He may take a short hop step or rhythm step before making the throw instead of taking a normal three-step drop.
- He may not find the laces of the football before making the throw.

Obviously, this type of passing game must be practiced. It is unnatural for a quarterback to receive the ball from the center, step into the throw, and pass the football without being able to grip the laces. At times the spiral will not be pretty; your main objective is to get the ball in the hands of the proper receiver in the most efficient manner possible.

Many times defenses will play off the receiver when you are in the shotgun formation because the odds are that you are going to throw the ball downfield. Not many offenses can or do throw the quick-passing game from the shotgun formation.

Five- and Seven-Step Drop-Pass Patterns Run from the Shotgun

When a pass play calls for a five-step, no-hitch drop – the corresponding drop from the shotgun in that same play will be two steps with a quick hitch-step. These patterns have pass routes that open up between 8 and 12-yards downfield. An example would be when the outside (primary) receivers are running 12-yard speed-outs.

When a play calls for a 5-big with a hitch-step drop, the corresponding shotgun drop is 4-quick with a quick hitch-step. These plays will have routes where the primary receiver will be breaking his route off at between 12 and 16-yards downfield, while at the same time the outside receiver on the two-receiver side is running a square-in route at 16-yards. The timing of the throws must timeout just as they would in a normal dropback pass.

In a normal seven-step dropback pattern, the routes are usually designed to open up beyond 15 yards downfield. The quarterback in the shotgun formation will then take four big steps in his drop before he hitches up to throw the pass.

It is also important to remember that during this *two- or four-step* drop phase in the shotgun formation, the quarterback still needs to have his shoulders slightly open to the line of scrimmage, just as he does in his normal drops. Too often quarterbacks will lose some of their mechanics in the shotgun formation because they are not used to it.

An excellent way to gage the correct timing of a shotgun drop is to line the shotgun quarterback along side of the quarterback directly behind the center. Have the ball snapped to both quarterbacks at the same time. Then both quarterbacks should drop back and end up throwing the ball at the same time. The timing should still be the same on all the routes.

One of the advantages to the shotgun formation is that the quarterbacks usually have a better sense of security because they are further from the line of scrimmage at the time of the snap from the center. Also, it is easier to see the whole field and, since the offensive receivers are spread out more, the reads are a bit easier for the quarterback to see.

One of the disadvantages to the shotgun formation is that it limits your play calls. You can't run all of your running plays from this formation. Another disadvantage is that young quarterbacks sometimes get used to this formation, and then their confidence in lining up behind the center dissipates at times. You probably shouldn't introduce the shotgun formation to your quarterbacks until they have mastered, and are comfortable with, dropping back in a normal fashion.

Summary of Shotgun Passing

- Running the offense from the shotgun formation usually makes the quarterback's job easier with respect to the passing game.
- The quarterback has a better vantage point from the shotgun.
- The shotgun formation limits the offense as far as what plays can be run.
- The shotgun formation can take away the rhythm and timing of some offenses.
- The stance is very important; the right foot should be back (in a right-handed quarterback).

- The quick-passing game can still be thrown from the shotgun.
- The quarterback doesn't have time to throw with the laces.
  - √   The *no-laces* throw must be practiced every day.
- The quarterback's normal drops should correspond to his shotgun drops.
- The quarterback's timing can still be attained from the shotgun.
- The various shotgun drops need to be practiced and refined.

CHAPTER 7

Play-Action Passing

Introduction

Using play action appropriately is one of the best weapons in your arsenal of offensive football plays. However, since this type of play is a bit more complex, time should be taken to teach it to the entire offense. It must be practiced on a daily basis so its mechanics are fundamentally sound and the execution is precise.

The linemen must understand that, at least at the point of attack, they must make contact at the line of scrimmage, rather that retreat into a normal pass-protection mode. This means that the play-action blocking is not as sound and can break down. The quarterback should be aware that there may be some penetration, and that he may take a hit just after the throw.

The running backs must run the same course they normally would on the running play, and must continue the fake as they pass through the line of scrimmage. The quarterback must take the same path and execute the same motions as he normally would on the running play until the very last second when he needs to look downfield and throw the football. All of these elements must be carried out with precision for the play to be most effective.

The quarterback should be expected to know and use three types of play-action fakes. The *A fake* is a fake where the quarterback must do his best to make the play look like exactly like a running play for a sustained period. The *B fake* is a type of fake where the quarterback will show the defense the football for a short time before pulling the ball back in and getting set to throw. The *C fake* is an action that quickly shows the defense the football, but does not affect the rhythm of a timing pattern.

Before a play-action pass is designed, it's important for the quarterback to understand what the play is supposed to do. First, whom do you want to influence (fake) with the play action? Is it one of the safeties, a cornerback, an outside linebacker, or an inside linebacker? Second, what running play will you be running your play-action pass off of? Third, what type of play fake is needed for the type of play you are designing? For example, when watching films of your opponent, which of the defenders is susceptible to the play fake? How does he react to the running play that your play-action pass is designed off of?

The A Fake

You should start with the A fake. An A fake is one where you want to do the best job fooling the defense. The A fake is the one where you want to get the back tackled; you want it to be a great fake (Figure 7-1). You want this action to appear identical to the run in every way until the last tenth of a second.

Figure 7-1. The A fake: The quarterback has the ball on his hip hidden from the defender(s) you want to deceive.

An example when this type of fake can be used is against a team whose safeties are responsible for run support – a type of *quarters* coverage. An appropriate play-action pass would most likely be built around an ISO play (a play where the full back will lead through the hole, and the tail back will follow with the ball). This deceptive play should be the type of play that will have an aggressive run-support safety coming up hard to the line of scrimmage when he reads *run*. This is a good opportunity to use a play that has your wide receiver running a post route (from the same side the play fake is run to). The safety will come up a bit as he reads run, and will then be out of position to cover the post (Figure 7-2).

Figure 7-2.

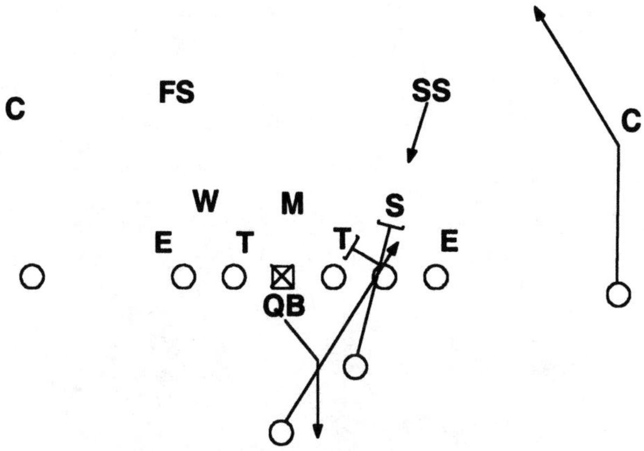

The quarterback should make the play-action fake look exactly like the original ISO play for a sustained period of time. As he takes the snap from center, he must pull the ball to his midsection. As he then moves to the faking back, the ball will stay at that level. The quarterback will locate the faking back and should look at the back's midsection – the area where he must place the football. He will then extend the ball with both hands to the back so that it is directly in front of him, clearly showing an exchange is imminent.

Now, as the ball is being pulled back to the quarterback's body with the off hand, the arm normally used to give the ball to the running back must be allowed to swing away, as it would if the quarterback had actually given the ball to the faking back. At the same time, the quarterback will take a peak at the back of that hand as his arm swings away in the same direction as the running back; this completes the fake. The ball should then be on the quarterback's back hip, hidden from the defense. It is important to have a coach watch the ball placement while standing 10 yards in front of the fake during practice time. Make sure the defense won't be able to see the ball while the quarterback has it hidden on his back hip.

Once the quarterback has completed the fake, he should bring the ball up into good a carriage position, and locate his receiver immediately as he hitches up to throw the pass. In a play-action pass, the quarterback doesn't have a lot of time to find all of his possible receivers. If the quarterback does not have his primary receiver, he must move up in the pocket and find an outlet receiver, or take off with the football.

The running back is also an important key in this type of play action. He must carry out the fake and, if it is a short-yardage play fake, dive to the ground. If this is an open-field play fake, his fake should be so convincing that the defense should tackle him. If fact, that should be the goal of the back, to be tackled because of the fake he has performed.

The B Fake

The B fake is a little different in that you still want to deceive the defense, but you are a little less concerned with hiding the ball for a sustained time period. You want to show the ball to the defense and bait them into flowing to where they think the play is going, then peel off and go the other way (Figure 7-3).

Figure 7-3. The B fake: The quarterback is showing the football to the defense before pulling it in and reversing the other way.

A good example of this would be a play where you want the defense to think you are running an outside stretch play to one side of the field, and then reverse out of that, and throw to the other side of the field (Figure 7-4).

As the quarterback receives the snap from the center, he will immediately place the ball in his midsection as he normally would during a run play. Then he will extend the football to the back (either with both hands or one hand) and hold the ball out so the whole defense can see it. While the quarterback meshes with the running back, he should have the ball held directly in front of the back establishing the likelihood of the exchange. The quarterback will then pull the ball back, snap his head around, and boot in the other direction (getting at least nine-yards depth from the line of scrimmage) and locate his primary receiver. He should have both hands on the football. As the quarterback prepares to throw the pass, he should put himself in a position to run directly towards the area where he wants the football to go. His hips should be square to his target and he should relax and exhale just as he is throwing the football.

Figure 7-4.

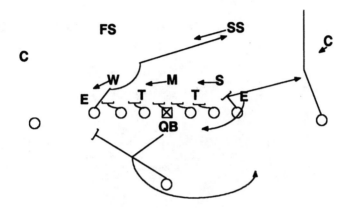

It is usually important that the quarterback understand several points when throwing on the run:

- You should run toward the target. This improves the accuracy of the throw, and keeps your hips square to the target.

- If you are throwing the ball at the receiver's feet, try standing up a little straighter just as you are ready to throw the pass. This helps to keep your shoulders more level during the throw.

- If you are consistently throwing the ball high to the receiver, you may have to lean forward slightly as you throw the pass.

- You should relax and exhale as your throw the football. This helps you keep your upper body and shoulders from tensing up as you throw the football.

- Be sure you don't overgrip the football. You should have a firm grip on the football, but gripping it too tightly will cause the ball to wobble, and you will lose some control.

- You should never throw across your body. You will lose a great deal of control and velocity on the pass, which will make it easier to intercept.

- You should never, ever, throw late over the middle. Most of the time, when you are lucky, the ball will fall incomplete. Often though, this is when interceptions occur.

The C Fake

The C fake is used on timing patterns, as well as to influence or *freeze* the one defender who you want to take out of the passing lane. This can almost be called a token fake. On this type of fake, you will flash the football to the defender as you drop back to pass, but you will quickly bring the ball back into your body so you can hit your last step and get rid of the football on time (Figure 7-5).

Figure 7-5. The C fake: You want to flash the ball at the defender, but not disrupt the timing of your pass.

Figure 7-6.

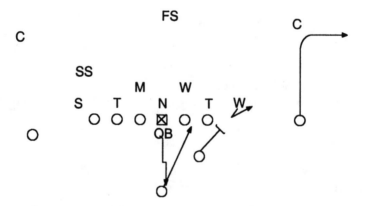

An example of this type of pass would be when you want to throw a 12-yard speed-out to your wide receiver on the weakside of the formation, but the outside linebacker has a tendency to fly to the flat and get into your passing lane. In this case, you will play action a back in his direction and flash the football at him. The linebacker will then hesitate (this is all you want) and you will be able to throw the ball before he retreats into your passing lane (Figure 7-6).

It is important to remember that the C fake is designed to make a specific defender hesitate before dropping back so you can throw the ball behind him. The timing of the pass is critical and the fake itself is a token fake. You just want to flash the ball to the defender so he reacts to it. The C fake can also be used in the quick-passing game to get the backer out of the passing lane of a slant or a hitch route.

How to Install the Mechanics of the Play-Action Passing Game

Although this is predominantly a quarterback book, the play-action passing game is so important that it is appropriate to talk a little bit about the best way to install the mechanics effectively.

Have a video camera tape this drill about 10 to 15 yards from the line of scrimmage, facing the offense. Start with just the center, the quarterback, and the backs. Execute the running play that you are going to build the play-action pass play off of. Do this several times to make sure everyone is running the play with precision.

Now run the play-action pass play several times interspersed with the running play. When you watch the tape, you will be able to point out the subtle nuances that need to be polished so that the play-action pass play looks exactly like the running play from the defensive standpoint. Any parent with a video camera can help out, and it's a great way to really hone the quarterback's ballhandling skills, as well as the back's skills to carry out the deception (Figure 7-7).

Figure 7-7.

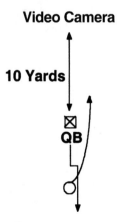

Summary of Play-Action Passing

- Play-action passing can be one of the best weapons in your offensive football arsenal.

- The plays themselves are more complex than strictly a running or a pass play, so all the members of the offensive team need to know what their roles are on the play.

- The linemen (at least at the point of attack) must make contact with the defender at the line of scrimmage, rather than to retreat in a pass-protection mode.

- The running backs must run the same course they normally would on the running play, and must continue the fake as they pass through the line of scrimmage.

- The quarterback must take the same path and execute the same motions as he normally would on the running play until the very last second when he needs to look downfield and throw the football.

- The quarterback must know whom he is trying to bait in the play-action pass.

- The three general types of play fakes are:

  √ The A fake – The quarterback does his best to make the play look exactly like the running play it was designed from.

  √ The B fake – The quarterback shows the ball to the defense, then pulls it back in and sets up to pass.

  √ The C fake – The quarterback quickly *flashes* the ball to a specific defender and continues in his drop to throw a timing pass.

CHAPTER 8

Rollout Passing Mechanics

Introduction

Rollout passing is a great way to disrupt the defensive rush techniques. Any quarterback should be able to do some type of rollout pass a few times a game as a change up from the dropback-type pass play, or the play- action type pass play.

The need for this technique is important because the quarterback needs to be in a good position with his hips as square to his target area as possible so he can throw an accurate pass with good velocity and rotation. The following two types of rollouts are the quick-roll type passes and the regular, deeper type rollout pass plays.

Quick-Roll Passing

The first step of the quarterback is one of the keys to an efficient rollout-type pass (Figure 8-1). With regard to the quick-roll pass, it may be necessary to get the ball up and out to the receiver as quickly as possible. These types of patterns tend to open up right away. One of the problems with this type of pass play is that the route has opened up and the quarterback is not able to get the ball to the receiver right away. This is usually because the quarterback is between strides, and doesn't feel ready to unload the ball. However, when a quarterback coach is cognizant of this, he and the quarterback can make the necessary adjustments, and correct this before it becomes a problem.

Figure 8-1. The quick roll: The quarterback on the left is on his third step and can either throw the pass or level out his path. The quarterback on the right is on his third step and will then level off.

An example of a quick-roll pass might be a flat route run by the primary receiver. The quarterbacks first step will be at a 45-degree angle (somewhere between four and five o'clock or seven and eight o'clock, as shown in Figure 8-2) in the direction he is rolling to. The step will resemble the same type of initial step a quarterback would take on an outside-stretch play.

Figure 8-2. This clock is a representation to be used when describing to the quarterback where, and at what angle, he should place his feet with respect to the running game, the play-action passing game, and the out-rollout passing game.

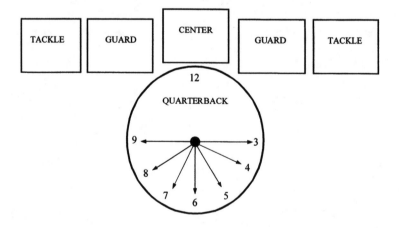

As the quarterback takes this initial step, he should bring the football up to a normal *carriage* position similar to the same position he would normally use on a dropback-type pass. His second step can be at the three or nine o'clock position if the play calls for him to get rid of the ball right away. At this point, his steps need to be shorter so the quarterback doesn't get caught between strides when he should be getting rid of the ball. He will be throwing the ball between his third and fourth step (going to his right) or his fourth and fifth steps (going to his left), or he will be leveling off and moving parallel to the line of scrimmage.

The quarterback should be throwing off the same foot he would in a dropback-type pass. If he is right handed, his right foot will be on the ground, and his left foot will be in front of him during the throw; he will push off his right foot to throw the pass.

The quarterback should get at least four-yards behind the line of scrimmage. This type of quick-roll pass is designed to get the ball to the receiver quickly. There will not be a lot time to wind up and throw the pass; this is more of a flick than a throw. This pass should be thrown more like a dart than a football (Figure 8-3).

As the quarterback throws this short pass, he should do his best to step where he wants the ball to go. This will square his hips to the target area. It is also important for the quarterback to remember two things as he throws the pass: first, relax as he brings the ball up and throws the pass; and second, breathe out. This will allow the quarterback's shoulders and arm to relax, and avoid a poor pass.

Figure 8-3.

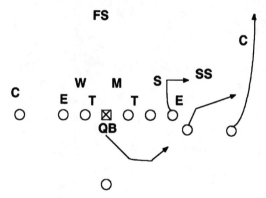

Summary of Quick-Roll Passing

* This type of pass play most often opens up right away.
* The quarterback's first step is critical.
* The quarterback's first step is taken at a 45-degree and is a fairly long stride, followed by shorter control-type steps.
* The quarterback will throw the pass off the same foot he normally would in a dropback-type pass.
* The quarterback should do his best to step toward the target area as he releases the ball.

Deep-Roll Passing

The normal rollout pass is designed to get the quarterback out of the pocket to throw the pass. Some teams have an audible where they will run away from an outside blitz with this type of play. Unlike the quick-roll pass, the quarterback is going to get much deeper (about nine yards from the line of scrimmage) before he turns upfield to throw the pass. His first step is going to be much closer to six o'clock so he can gain depth, away from the line of scrimmage, before leveling off and then stepping towards the target area (Figure 8-4).

Figure 8-4. The quarterback gains depth and separation on his first step in the deep-roll passing play.

As the quarterback gains depth, he will carry the ball much like he does in a dropback- pass mode. He must be relaxed and efficient with his movements. As he passes seven yards in depth, he will cut down his speed a little and get himself under control. He is virtually running towards the sideline at this point, and he then starts looking at his progression. After two to four strides, he will move back towards the line of scrimmage and his target area. It's important to remember that the quarterback's hips should be squared to the target area (where he wants the ball to end up). At this point, he will cut his speed so that he is totally under control. Again, much like the quick-roll pass, this is the point where he needs to shorten his steps to prevent getting caught between strides when he should be throwing the football. It is also important that he throws off the same foot he would in a dropback-pass situation. It is very hard to wind up for the throw – the pass should be thrown with a flick of the wrist (Figure 8-5).

Several things need to be addressed with regard to the deep-roll passing game. First, when a right-handed quarterback is rolling out to his left side, he needs to get a little deeper so that he can make sure he is able to square his hips to his target area before the throw. Second, the quarterback should be moving in the direction of the target area just before the throw. Third, it is safer to roll the quarterback to his left than his right. The reason being that when a quarterback rolls to his right, throws, and is hit by a defender, he will be driving his throwing shoulder into the ground. If the quarterback finds himself in this defenseless position, he should do all he can to roll into the tackle and land squarely on his back, to avoid landing on his throwing shoulder.

Finally, this rollout type movement needs to be practiced every day, even if it's only a warm-up drill, to ensure that the quarterback uses the proper mechanics for efficiency and accuracy. When the *bullets are flying*, all these mechanics tend to break down.

Figure 8-5.

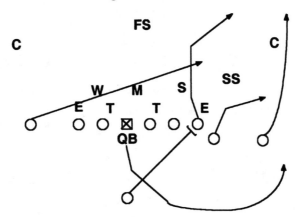

Summary of Deep-Roll Passing

- The quarterback should get about nine yards in depth.
- The quarterback's first step is at about six-o'clock.
- The quarterback should carry the ball in a normal carriage position.
- The quarterback should start to level off at about seven-yards deep from the line of scrimmage.
- As the quarterback gets ready to throw, he should start to move to the target area under control.
- The quarterback should then shorten his strides a bit so he doesn't get caught between strides.
- The quarterback should remember to get a little deeper drop when throwing to his offside.
- If the quarterback is about to get hit as he is rolling to his right (right-handed quarterback) he should try to land square on his back, rather than his throwing shoulder.

DRILL #12: THROW-AT-THE-TARGET-AREA-ON-THE-RUN DRILL

Objective: To teach the mechanics necessary to throw an accurate pass on the run with your hips squared to your target.

Equipment Needed: One football

Description: The quarterback will line up 10 to 15 yards away from the receiver. This distance can be extended as the quarterback learns the techniques of throwing on the run. The quarterback will start by jogging at the receiver and throwing the pass with the proper mechanics (Figure 8-6).

Coaching Points:

- The quarterback will square his hips to the target as he throws the pass.
- The quarterback will throw off the proper foot using sound throwing mechanics.
- If the pass is inaccurate or does not have the proper rotation, the distance should be shortened.

Skill Simulated: Throwing *waggle-* or *bootleg-*type passes, and/or throwing on the run (Figure 8-7).

Figure 8-6.　　　　　**Figure 8-7.**

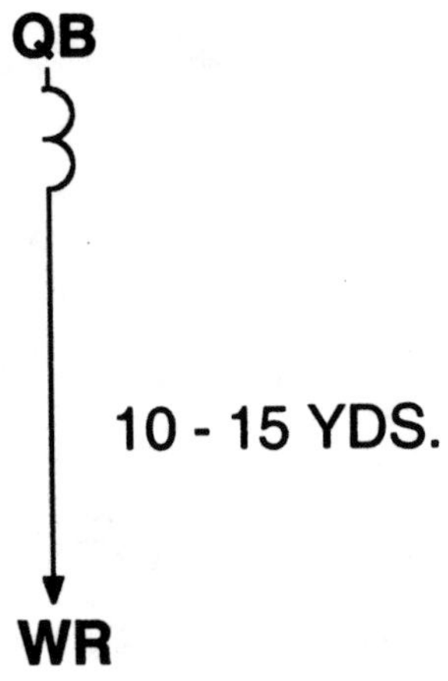

QB

10 - 15 YDS.

WR

This is an example of good technique. The quarterback threw the ball with his right foot on the ground and his left foot in front of him. He threw it like a dart, and the ball has good rotation on it. His hips and shoulders are squared to the target area at the time of the throw.

DRILL #13: THE CIRCLE DRILL

Objective: To teach the mechanics necessary to throw an accurate pass on the run.

Equipment Needed: One football, football cleats, and a lined field

Description: The quarterbacks will line up 10 to 15 yards apart from each other. They will start to jog in a clockwise (and then counter-clockwise) direction. They will throw the ball to each other during this time. This will simulate throwing on the run (Figure 8-8).

Coaching Points:

- The quarterbacks will square their hips to the target as they throw the pass.
- The quarterbacks will exercise proper follow-through mechanics.

Skill Simulated: Throwing *waggle-* or *bootleg-*type passes, and/or throwing on the run.

Figure 8-8.

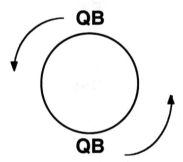

CHAPTER 9

Contingency Plans in the Passing Game

Introduction

Many times during a football game, a quarterback will drop back, and for one reason of another, the protection breaks down, or he can't find anyone open. In these cases, the quarterback has several choices. First, he can throw the ball away, which stops the clock. There are times when this is the appropriate decision. Second, he can take the sack, which keeps the clock running. There are times when this is the correct choice. Third, the quarterback can go to a contingency plan, and make a play downfield.

The receiver will run his route, make his break, and create separation from the defender. The receiver realizes that the quarterback is taking off laterally. This is when the receiver has to make the appropriate adjustment – *the contingency plan*.

The Contingency Plan in the Dropback-Passing Game

When a pass play breaks down, the receivers should run to specific areas on the field to form a *triangle of opportunity* for the quarterback. The receivers should make the appropriate adjustments. The widest receiver to the side the quarterback is moving to should take the deep area to that side. The inside receiver should slide at a depth between the line of scrimmage and the deepest receiver, and the receiver furthest from the quarterback should slide horizontally and slightly up field. As the quarterback rolls to one side or the other, he can keep the ball or throw to one of the receivers (Figure 9-1).

Figure 9-1.

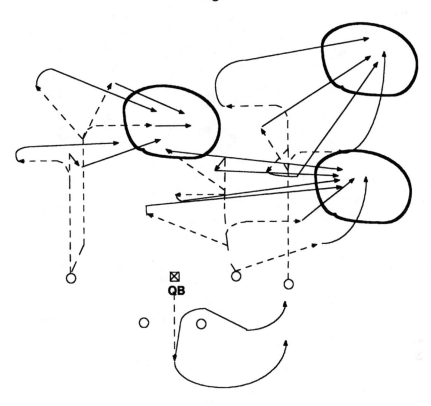

If running backs are involved in the play, they will also go to the appropriate open area. This type of contingency plan can create big plays. However, this type of plan should be practiced repeatedly for it to become second nature for the players (Figure 9-2).

The Contingency Plan in the Quick-Passing Game

In the quick-passing game, the quarterback has to lose ground and then slide horizontally. The receivers' basic rules are the same. The widest receiver to the side the quarterback is moving to should take the deep area to that side. The inside receiver should slide at a depth between the line of scrimmage and the deepest receiver, and the receiver furthest from the quarterback should slide horizontally and slightly up field (Figures 9-3 and 9-4).

Figure 9-2.

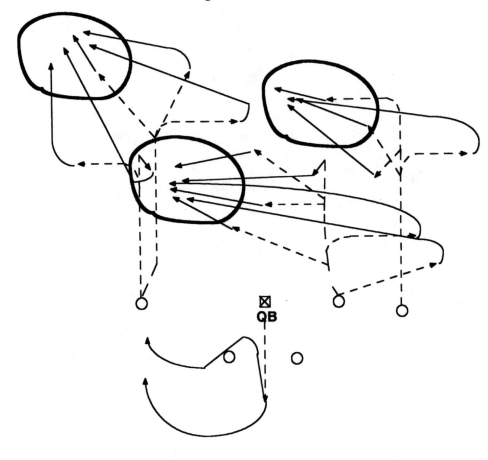

Figure 9-3.

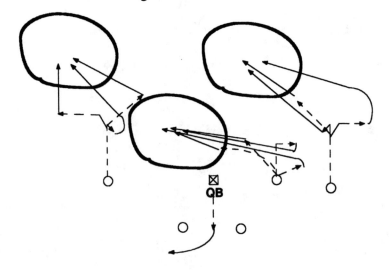

Figure 9-4.

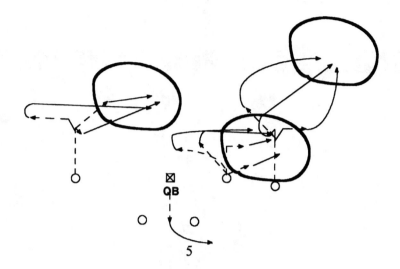

CHAPTER 10

Shifting and Putting Players in Motion

Introduction

Shifting and putting players in motion can help an offense do several important things. It can force the defense to make some type of adjustment – even if it a slight adjustment, which keeps the defense at bay. It can also give the offense an indicator of what coverage the defense is in.

Shifting is when usually more than one player moves from one set to another before the snap of the ball. The backs can come out of the backfield and line up as receivers, or the tight end can shift from one side of the formation to the other – and change the strength of the formation.

Motion occurs when all eleven players on offense have been in a set position for at least one second, and then only one player moves horizontally behind the line of scrimmage until the snap of the ball.

Shifting Players

The first thing to remember about shifting is that the quarterback is responsible to get the play called, and all of the offensive players to the line of scrimmage quickly. When a team utilizes shifting, there needs to be a sense of urgency about getting to the line of scrimmage as quickly as possible.

Second, the quarterback should be under the center before he shifts the players (usually with the word *go*). This is important because you want to appear to be the position you will be in when the ball is finally snapped. If the quarterback just stands behind the center and calls out the shift, it doesn't affect the defense very much. The shift should either slightly surprise the defense, or at least have them on *their heels* before the snap of the ball.

Third, all the players that shifted must be in a set position for at least one second before the ball is snapped, or before another offensive player goes in motion. It is the quarterback's responsibility to make sure everyone is set.

Figure 10-1 illustrates a shift. The tight end changes sides, thereby changing the strength of the formation. The backs shift from the backfield to *wing* positions. The defense first sees a somewhat normal, two-back formation that changes to an *empty* look.

Figure 10-1.

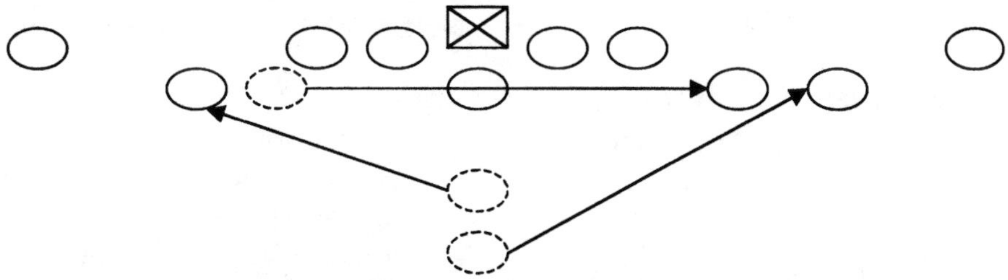

Motioning Players

A few important points need to be mentioned with respect to motioning. First, the offense needs to get to the line of scrimmage quickly. Second, the quarterback must make sure that all the shifting has been completed and that everyone is set for at least one second before the motioning back or receiver goes in motion. Third, the quarterback should receive the ball when the man in motion is where he is supposed to be to start the play. This takes practice and awareness from the quarterback. The receiver should move to the area he will be in when the ball is to be snapped, and then slow down a bit so the quarterback has time to synchronize his snap-count (Figure 10-2).

Figure 10-2.

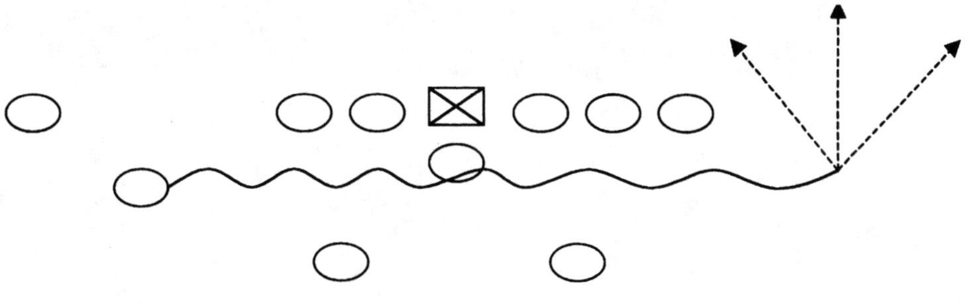

An exception would be if the receiver is going to run some kind of *rub* route, it is sometimes beneficial to get out of the backfield as quickly as possible, even if that momentum takes him slightly outside with no real threat of breaking back against the grain to run a route to the inside of the field (Figure 10-3).

Figure 10-3.

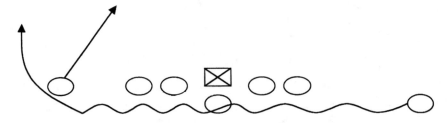

In addition, the quarterback should pay close attention to how the defense reacts to the motioning. If a man is running with the motioning player, it is some type of man coverage. If the defense *bumps* or shifts slightly, it is usually some type of zone.

To put a player in motion, the quarterback must first make sure everyone on offense has been is a set position for at least one second. Then the quarterback should take his foot and tap it in the backfield about 12-inches behind him, to the side the motion man is on. If the motion man is on the quarterback's right side, the quarterback will tap with his right foot. If the motion man is on the quarterback's left side, the quarterback will then reach his left foot back to put him in motion (Figures 10-4 and 10-5).

Figure 10-4. This is the motion man going in motion starting from the quarterback's right side.

Figure 10-5. This is an example from the perspective of the man going in motion from the left of the quarterback.

Motioning and shifting should be practiced every week, and they should be isolated drills. It is wasting valuable practice time learning how to shift and go in motion when a play, or series of plays is being installed. You should practice shifting and motioning at least 5 to 10 minutes at the beginning of each practice week.

CHAPTER 11

Quarterback-Technique Warm-Ups and Drills

Warm-Ups
(used to loosen players up and teach good form)

Throwing on Both Knees:
- The quarterback will be on both knees and will throw using good form.
- This forces the quarterback to throw with the proper motion.
- This loosens up his trunk and shoulder areas.

Throwing from a Squared-Up, Standing Position:
- The quarterback will have his feet approximately shoulder-width apart with most of his weight on the balls of his feet.
- This forces the quarterback to throw with the proper motion.

Bullpen Throws:
The quarterback will throw from the stretch position (just like a pitcher would).
This teaches follow-through and form.

Easy Ups:
- This teaches *touch* and works the feet.
- This forces the ball to turn over before it gets to the receiver.

Drills
(used to teach the exact technique that would be used in a game situation)

Going Through Each Individual Drop:
- This is the most important drill in the offense.
- The coach will have the different drop depths marked on the field.
- A center or *Sure-snap* machine is needed.
- The coach will stand where the receivers would catch the ball in each route.
- The quarterback will start with the short throws and work to the deeper throws.
- The quarterback will go through the backside throws first.
- The quarterback will go through every route twice in a row.

Drops-At-Hot Drill:
- The quarterback will go through a five- and seven-step drop and yell *hot* to get him to pull up and throw an accurate pass with good velocity.
- The quarterback should work on throwing to the different areas of the field where the hot routes would normally be.

Hitch-Up-and-Throw Drill:
- The quarterback will start from the second to last step in his drop and work on his weight transfer.
- This teaches the quarterback to transfer his weight from moving backward to moving forward.
- This is an ideal drill to make the quarterback's hitch smooth and efficient.

Quick-Release Drill:
- The quarterback will stand in the stretch position and get rid of the ball as quickly, smoothly, and as accurately as he can.
- You will have your quarterbacks compete against each other.
- You will have the targets stand about 10 to 15 yards away from the quarterback.

Drop-and-Throw with a High-Release Drill:
- This is to simulate a screen with no rushers.
- This teaches the quarterbacks rhythm that is necessary on screens.

Hitch-Up-and-Escape Drill:
- This is necessary for contingency plans when a play breaks down.
- You will have the quarterback drop back, hitch-up in the pocket twice, and take off towards the side he is reading.
- The quarterback will square his hips and make a good accurate throw at a target.
- The quarterback needs to relax and breathe out just as he is making the throw.

Man-in-the-Middle Drill:
- You will place two receivers where they would be at the end of their complimentary routes (curl – flat or dig – drag).
- You will put a defender in position to cover both routes.
- You will have the quarterback take his normal drop and hit one of the receivers.
- The quarterback is allowed to look off the defender.
- The quarterback is not allowed to pump fake.
- The quarterback must get rid of the ball on time.
- This teaches the quarterback to look off defenders.
- This teaches the quarterback to have a faster release.

Play-Action Drill:
- You will put a receiver where he would be catching the pass on a specific play.
- You will have a back go through his play fake.
- The quarterback should appear to be giving the ball to the back with both hands on the ball while looking the ball into the back's stomach area.
- As the back passes, the quarterback should pull the ball back (with his right hand) and place the ball on his back hip.
  - √ A coach should stand at the line of scrimmage to make sure the quarterback is hiding the ball.
- The quarterback should follow through with his left hand and allow it to swing up (as it normally would during an actual handoff) as he finds his receiver downfield.
- As the quarterback hits the end of his drop, he should bring the ball up to a good throwing position and be able to deliver the ball on time in an efficient throwing motion.

Waggle Drill:

- You will have the quarterback take the snap from the center and roll out to one side or the other and throw to the different routes.
- You should stress the importance of relaxing and breathing out just as the quarterback throws the pass on the run.

Dash Drill:

- You will have the quarterback drop back seven steps.
- The quarterback needs to be patient and let the rush come to him.
- At the appropriate time, the quarterback will wheel around (moving to his backside), or step at a 45-degree angle (moving to his frontside), and throw the appropriate pass.
- You should stress the importance of relaxing and breathing out just as the quarterback throws the pass on the run.

Fade Drill with a Trashcan:

- You will have the quarterback stand at various points between the hash marks.
- You will place a trashcan at a point downfield to simulate where a receiver would catch the pass on a fade and on a streak.
- This teaches the quarterback to get the ball to turn over.
- This teaches the quarterback to put touch on the pass.

Routes-vs.-Air Drill:

- This is a great drill for working on timing.
- The quarterbacks and receivers will start off at half speed and both should have near perfect technique.
   √   Whenever you run half speed, the technique should be emphasized.
- This also teaches the quarterback to know where all the routes are.